(ASRAR-I-KHUDI)

creators other than God XIV
Queran Chap, V. 14

Solipsism
syndrome خودی کا .

معین الدین ۔ اجمیر
خواجری ۔ الٰہ } 71

War is good 88

THE SECRETS
OF
THE SELF

(ASRAR-I-KHUDI)

A PHILOSOPHICAL POEM

by
DR. SIR MUHAMMAD IQBAL

Translated from the original Persian
with Introduction and Notes
by
REYNOLD A NICHOLSON
LITT. D. LL.D.

Lecturer on Persian in the University of Cambridge

kitaB BhaVan
NEW DELHI-110 002. [INDIA]

Kitab Bhavan
Publishers, Distributors, Exporters & Importers
1784, Kalan Mahal, Darya Ganj
New Delhi-110002 (India)

Phone	:	(91-11)23277392/93,23274686
Website	:	www.kitabbhavan.com
E-Mail	:	nasri@vsnl.com
Fax	:	(91-11) 23263383

ISBN 81-7151-250-X

Improved Edition 2000
Reprinted............2004

Laser Typesetting at:
Laser Track,
1784, Kalan Mahal Drya Ganj
New Delhi-110002 (India)

Published in India By:
Nusrat Ali Nasri for Kitab Bhavan
1784, kalan Mahal Drya Ganj
New Delhi-110002 (India)

Printed in India at:
Lahooti Fine Art Press
1711, Sui Walan, Darya Ganj
New Delhi-110002 (India)

C ONTENTS

INTRODUCTION

The *Asrar-i-Khudi* was first published at Lahore in 1915. I read it soon afterwards and thought so highly of it that I wrote to Iqbal, whom I had the pleasure of meeting at Cambridge some fifteen years ago, asking leave to prepare an English translation. My proposal was cordially accepted, but in the meantime I found other work to do, which caused the translation to be laid aside until last year. Before submiyting it to the reader, a few remarks are necessary concerning the poem and its author.[1]

Iqbal is an Indian Muslim. During his stay in the West he studied modern philosophy, in which subjects he holds degrees from the Universities of Cambridge and Munich. His dissertation on the development of metaphysics in Persia—an illuminating sketch-appeared as a book in 1908. Since then he has developed a philosophy of his own, on which I am able to give some extremely interesting notes communicated by himself. Of this, however, the *Asrar-i-Khudi* gives no systematic account, though it

---

1. The Present translation follows the text of the second edition.

puts his ideas in a popular and attractive form. While
the Hindu philosophers, in explaining the doctrine of
the unity of being, addressed themselves to the head,
Iqbal, like the Persian poets who teach the same
doctrine, takes a more dangerous course and aims at
the heart. He is no mean poet, and his verse can rouse
or persuade even if his logic fails to convince. His
message is not for the Mohammedans of India alone,
but for Muslims everywhere: accordingly he writes
in Persian instead of Hindustani— a happy choice,
for amongst educated Muslims there are many familiar
with Persian literature, while the Persian language is
singularly well-adapted to express philosophical ideas
in a style at once elevated and charming.

Iqbal comes forward as an apostle, if not to his
own age, then to posterity—

"I have no need of the ear of To-day.

I am the voice of the poet of To-morrow"—

and after Persian fashion he invokes the Saki to
fill his cup with wine and pour moonbeams into the
dark night of his thought.

"That I may lead home the wanderer.
And imbue the idle looker-on with restless impatience.
And advance hotly on a new quest.
And become known as the champion of a new spirit."

Let us begin at the end. What is the far-off goal on

which his eyes are fixed? The answer to that question will discover his true character, and we shall be less likely to stumble on the way if we see whither we are going. Iqbal has drunk deep of European literature, his philosophy owes much to Nietzsche and Bergson, and his poetry, often remains us of Shelly; yet he thinks and feels as a Muslim, and just for this reason his influence may be great. He is a religious enthusiast, inspired by the vision of New Makkah, a world-wide, theocratic, Utopian state in which all Muslims, no longer divided by the barriers of race and country, shall be one. He will have nothing to do with nationalism and imperialism. These, he says, "rob us of Paradise": they make us strangers to each other, destroy feelings of brotherhood, and sow the bitter seed of war. He dreams of a world ruled by religion, not by politics and condemns Machiavelli, that "worshipped of false goods," who has blinded so many. It must be observed that when he speaks of religion he always means Islam. Non-Muslims are simply unbelievers, and (in theory, at any rate) the Jihād is justifiable, provided that it is wages "for God's sake alone." A free and independent Muslim fraternity, having the Ka'ba as its centre and knit together by love of Allah and devotion to the Prophet—such is Iqbal's ideal. In the *Asrar-i-Khudi* and the *Rumuz-i-*

Bekhudi he preaches it with a burning sincerity which we cannot but admire, and at the same time points out how it may be attained. The former poem deals with the life of the individual Muslim, the latter with the life of the Islamic community.

The cry "Back to the Qur'ān! Back to Muhammad! has been heard before, and the responses have hitherto been somewhat discouraging. But on this occasion it is allied with the revolutionary force of Western philosophy, which Iqbal hopes and believes will vitalise the movement and ensure its triumph. He sees that Hindu intellectualism and Islamic pantheism have destroyed the capacity for action, based on scientific observation and interpretation of phenomena, which distinguishes the Western peoples "and especially the English." Now, this capacity depends ultimately on the conviction that *Khudi* (selfhood, individuality, personality) is real and is not merely an illusion of the mind. Iqbal, therefore, throws himself with all his might against idealistic philosophers and pseudo-mystical poets, the authors, in his opinion, of the decay prevailing in Islam, and argues that only by self-affirmation, self-expression, and self-development can the Muslims once more become strong and free. He appeals from the alluring raptures of Hafiz to the moral fervour of Jalalu'd din Rumi, from an Islam sunk in Platonic contemplation to the fresh and vigorous monotheism which inspired Muhammad and brought Islam into existence.[2] Here, perhaps, I should guard against a possible misunderstanding. Iqbal's philosophy is religious, but he does not treat philosophy as the handmaid of religion. Holding that the full development of the individual presupposes a society, he finds the ideal society in what he considers to be the Prophet's conception of Islam. Every Muslim, in striving to make himself a more perfect individual, is helping to establish the Islamic kingdom of God upon earth.[3]

The *Asrar-i-Khudi* is composed in the meter and modelled on the style of the famous *Masnavi*. In the prologue Iqbal relates how Jalalu'ddin Rumi, who is

---

2. His criticism of Hafiz called forth angry protests from Sufi circles in which Hafiz is venerated as a master-hierophant. Iqbal made no recantation, but since the passage had served its purpose and was offensive to many, he cancelled it in the second edition of the poem. It is omitted in my translation.

3. The principles of Islam, regarded as the ideal society, are set forth in the author's second poem, the *Rumuz-i-Bekhudi* or "Mysteries of Selflessness." He explains the title by pointing out that the individual who loses himself in the community reflects both the past and the future as in a mirror, so that he transcends morality and enters into that life of Islam, which is infinite and everlasting. Among the topics discussed are the origin of society, the divine guidance of man through the prophets, the formation of collective life-centres, and the value of History as a factor in maintaining the sense of personal entity in a people.

to him almost what Virgil was to Dante, appeared in a
vision and bade him arise and sing. Much as he dislikes
the type of Sufism exhibited by Hafiz, he pays homage
to the pure and profound genius of Jalalu'ddin, though
he rejects the doctrine of self-abandonment taught by
the great Persian mystic and does not accompany him
in his pantheistic flights.

To European readers the *Asrar-i-Khudi* presents
certain obscurities which no translation can entirely
remove. These lie partly in the form and would not be
felt, as a rule, by any one conversant with Persian
poetry. Often, however, the ideas themselves, being
associated with peculiarly Oriental ways of thinking,
are hard for our minds to follow. I am not sure that I
have always grasped the meaning or rendered it
correctly; but I hope that such errors are few, thanks
to the assistance so kindly given me by my friend
Muhammad Shafi, now Professor of Arabic at Lahore,
with whom I read the poem and discussed many points
of difficulty. Other questions of a more fundamental
character have been solved for me by the author
himself. At my request he drew up a statement of his
philosophical views on the problems touched and
suggested in the book. I will give it in his own words
as nearly as possible. It is not, of course, a complete
statement, and was written, as he says, "in a great

hurry," but apart from its power and originality it elucidates the poetical argument far better than any explanation that could have been offered by me.

1. THE PHILOSOPHICAL BASIS OF THE *ASRAR-I-KHUDI*

" 'The experience should take place in finite centres and should wear the form of finite this-ness is in the end inexplicable.' These are the words of Prof. Bradley. But starting with these inexplicable centres of experience, he ends in a unity which he calls Absolute and in which the finite centres lose their finiteness and distinctness. According to him, therefore, the finite centre is only an appearance. The test of reality, in his opinion is all-inclusiveness; and since all finiteness is 'infected with relativity,' it follows that the latter is a mere illusion. To my mind, this inexplicable finite centre of experience is the fundamental fact of the universe. All life is individual; there is no such thing as universal life. God himself is an individual: He is the most unique individual.[4] The universe, as Dr. McTaggart says, is an association of individuals; but we must add that the orderliness and adjustment which we find in this association is not

---

4. This view was held by the orthodox Imam Ahmad Ibn Hanbal in its extreme (anthropomorphic) form.

eternally achieved and complete in itself. It is the result of instinctive or conscious effort. We are gradually travelling from chaos to cosmos and are helpers in this achievement. Nor are the members of the association fixed; new members are ever coming to birth to co-operate in the great task. Thus the universe is not a completed act: it is still in the course of formation. There can be no complete truth about the universe, for the universe has not yet become 'whole.' The process of creation is still going, on, and man too takes his share in it, inasmuch as he helps to bring order into at least a portion of the chaos. The Qur'ān indicates the possibility of other creators than God.[5]

"Obviously this view of man and the universe is opposed to that of the English Neo-Hegelians as well as to all forms of pantheistic Sufism which regard absorption in a universal life or soul as the final aim and salvation of man.[6] The moral and religious ideal of man is not self-negation but self-affirmation, and he attains to this ideal by becoming more and more individual, more and more unique. The Prophet said, '*Takhallaqu bi-akhlaq Allah*,' 'Create in yourselves the attributes of God.' Thus man becomes unique by becoming more and more like the most unique

---

5. Qur'ān, ch. 23, v. 14; "Blessed is God, the best of those who create."
6. Cf. his note on "Islam and Mysticism" (*The New Era*, 1916, p. 250)

Individual. What then is life? It is individual: its highest form, so far, is the Ego (*Khudi*) in which the individual becomes a self-contained exclusive centre. Physically as well as spiritually man is self-contained centre, but he is not yet a complete individual. The greater his distance from God, the less his individuality. He who comes nearest to God is the completes person. Nor that he is finally absorbed in God. On the contrary, he absorbs God into himself. [7] The true person not only absorbs the world of matter; by mastering it he absorbs God Himself into his Ego. Life is a forward assimilative movement. It removes all obstructions in its march by assimilating them. Its essence is the continual creation of desires and ideals, and for the purpose of it its preservation and expansion it has invented or developed out of itself certain

---

[7]. Here Iqbal adds; "Maulana Rumi has very beautifully expressed this idea. The Prophet, when a little boy, was once lost in the desert. His nurse Halima was almost beside herself with grief but while roaming the desert in search of the boy she heard a voice saying:

'Do not grieve, he will not be lost to thee;

Nay, the whole world will be lost in him.'

The true individual cannot be lost in the world; it is the world that is lost in him. I go a step further and say, prefixing a new half-verse to a hemistich of Rumi (Trans. I, 1325);

In his will that which God wills becomes lost.

'How shall a man believe this saying?"

* ساز بے پہلو سے درد و سوز آرزو مندی
مقام بندگی دے کر نہ لوں شان خداوندی (اقبال)

instruments, e.g., senses, intellect, etc., which help in to assimilate obstruction.[8] The greatest obstacle in the way of life is matter, Nature; yet Nature is not evil, since it enables the inner powers of life to unfold themselves.

"The Ego attains to freedom by the removal of all obstructions in its way. It is partly free, partly determined,[9] and reaches fuller freedom by approaching the Individual who is most free—God. In one word, life is an endeavour for freedom.' "

2. THE EGO AND CONTINUATION OF PERSONALITY

"In man the centre of life becomes an Ego or Person. Personality is a state of tension and can continue only if that state is maintained. If the state of tension is not maintained, relaxation will ensue. Since personality, or the state of tension, is the most valuable achievement of man, he should see that he does not revert to a state of relaxation. That which tends to maintain the state of tension tends to make us immortal. Thus the idea of personality gives us a

---

8. Transl. 1, 289 foll.
9. According to the Tradition, "The true Faith is between predestination of free-will."

and

standard of value: it settles the problem of good and evil. That which fortifies personality is good, that which weakens it is bad. Art,[10] religion, and ethics[11] must be judged from the 'stand-point of personality. My criticism of Plato[12] is directed against those philosophical systems which hold up death rather than life as their ideal—systems which ignore the greatest obstruction to life, namely, matter and teach us to run away from it instead of absorbing it.

"As in connection with the question of the freedom of the Ego we have to face the problem of matter, similarly in connection with its immorality we have to face the problem of time.[13] Bergson has taught us that time is not an infinite line (in the spatial sense of

---

10. Transl. 1. 673 foll. In a note on "Our Prophet's criticism of contemporary Arabian poetry" (*The New Era*, 1916, p. 251) Iqbal writes: "The ultimate end of all human activity is Life—glorious, powerful, exuberant. All human art must be subordinated to this final purpose, and the value of everything must be determined in reference to its life-yielding capacity. The highest art is that which awakens our dormant will-force and nerves us to face the trials of life manfully. All that brings drowsiness and makes us shut our eyes to Reality around, on the mastery of which alone Life depends, is a message of decay and death. There should be no opiumeating in Art. The dogma of Art for the sake of Art is a clever invention of decadence to cheat us out of life and power."

11. Ibid, 1. 537 foll.

12. Ibid, I, 631 foll.

13. Transal. I. 1531 foll.

cruel, destructive, mad

the word 'line') through which we must pass whether we wish it or not. This idea of time is adulterated. Pure time has no length. Personal immorality is an aspiration: you can have it if you make an effort to achieve it. It depends on our adopting in this life modes of thought and activity which tend to maintain the state of tension. Buddhism, Persian Sufism and allied forms of ethics will not serve our purpose. But they are not wholly useless, because after periods of great activity we need opiates, narcotics, for some time. These forms of thought and action are like nights in the days of life. Thus, if our activity is directed towards the maintenance of a state of tension, the shock of death is not likely to affect it. After death there may be an interval of relaxation, as the Qur'ān speaks of a *barzakh*, or intermediate state, which lasts until the Day of Resurrection.[14] Only those Egos will survive this state of relaxation who have taken good care during the present life. Although life abhors repetition in its evolution, yet on Bergson's principles the resurrection of the body too, as Wildon Carr says, is quite possible. By breaking up time into moments we spatialise it and then find difficulty in getting over it. The true nature of time is reached when we look into

---

14. Qur'ān, ch. 23, v. 102.

our deeper self.[15] Real time is life itself which can preserve itself by maintaining that particular state of tension (personality) which it has so far achieved. We are subject to time so long as we look upon time as something special. Specialised time is a fetter which life has forged for itself in order to assimilate the present environment. In reality we are timeless, and it is possible to realise our timelessness even in this life. This revelation, however, can be momentary only.

3. THE EDUCATION OF THE EGO

"The Ego is fortified by love (Ishq).[16] This word is used in a very wide sense and means the desire to assimilate, to absorb. Its highest form is the creation of values and ideals and the endeavour to realise them. Love individualises the lover as well as the beloved. The effort to realise the most unique individuality individualises the seeker and implies the individuality of the sought, for nothing else would satisfy the nature of the seeker. As love fortifies the Ego, asking (sua'l) weakens it.[17] All that is achieved without personal effort comes under sua'l. The son of a rich man who inherits his father's wealth is an 'asker' (beggar); so is every one who thinks the thoughts of others. Thus, in order to fortify the Ego we should cultivate love,

15. Transl. 1. 1549 foll.
16. Transl. 1. 323 foll.
17. Transl. 1.435 foll.

+ getting assimilated (not destroyed)

i.e., the power of assimilative action, and avoid all forms of 'asking, *i.e.* inaction. The lesson of assimilative action is given by the life of the Prophet, at least to a Muhammadan."

"In another part of the poem[18] I have hinted at the general principles of Muslim ethics and have tried to reveal their meanings in connection with the idea of personality. The Ego in its movement towards uniqueness has to pass through three stages:

+ inclusiveness

(*a*) Obedience to the Law.

(*b*) Self-control, which is the highest form of self-consciousness or Ego-hood![19]

(*c*) Divine vicegerency [20]

"This (divine vicegerency, *niyabat-i-ilahi*), is the third and last stage of human development on earth. The *na'ib* (vicegerent) is the vicegerent of God on earth. He is the completest Ego, the goal of humanity,[21] the acume of life both in mind and body; in him the discord of our mental life becomes a harmony. This

---

18. *Ibid,* 1, 815 foll.

19. Transl. 1.849 foll.

20. *Ibid.* 1.893 foll

21. Man already possesses the germ of vicegerency, as God says in the Qur'ān (ch. 2, v. 28); "Lo I will appoint a *Khalifa* (vicegerent) on the earth." Cf. Transl, 1.434.

the Viceregent

highest power is united in him with the highest knowledge. In this life, thought and action, instinct and reason, become one. He is the last fruit of the tree of humanity, and all the trials of a painful evolution are justified because he is to come at the end. He is the real ruler of mankind; his kingdom is the kingdom of God on earth. Out of the richness of his nature he lavishes the wealth of life on others, and brings them nearer and nearer to himself. The more we advance in evolution, the nearer we got to him. In approaching him we are raising ourselves in the scale of life. The development of humanity both in mind and body is a condition precedent to his birth. For the present he is a mere ideal; but the evolution of humanity is tending towards the production of an ideal race of more or less unique individuals who will become his fitting parents. Thus the Kingdom of God on earth means the democracy of more or less unique individuals, presided over by the most unique individual possible on this earth. Nietzsche had a glimpse of this ideal race, but his atheism and aristocratic prejudices marred his whole conception."[22]

king

Every one, I suppose, will acknowledge that the

22. Writing of "Muslim Democracy" in *The New Era*, 1916, p. 251, Iqbal says: "The Democracy of Europe—fear overshadowed by socialistic agitation and anarchical—originated mainly in the economic

(Contd. next page)

substance of the *Asrar-i-Khudi* is striking enough to command attention. In the poem, naturally, this philosophy presents itself under a different aspect. Its audacity of thought and phrase is less apparent, its logical brilliancy dissolves in the glow of feeling and imagination, and it wins the heart before taking possession of the mind. The artistic quality of the poem is remarkable when we consider that its language is not the author's own. I have done my best to preserve as much of this as a literal prose translation would allow. Many passages of the original are poetry of the kind that, once read, is not easily forgotten, *e.g.,* the description of the Ideal Man as a deliverer for whom the word is waiting, and the noble invocation which brings the book to an end. Like Jalalu'ddin Rumi, Iqbal is fond of introducing fables and apologues to relieve the argument and illustrate his meaning with more force and point than would be possible otherwise.

---

regeneration of European societies. Nietzsche, however, abhors this 'rule, of the heard and, hopeless of the plebeian, he bases all higher culture on the cultivation and growth of an Aristocracy of Supermen. But is the plebeian so absolutely hopeless? The Democracy of Islam did not grow out of the extension of economic opportunity; it is a spiritual principle based on the assumption that every human being is a centre of latent power the possibilities of which can be developed by cultivating a certain type of character. One of the plebeian material Islam has formed men of the noblest type of life and power. Is not, then, the Democracy of early Islam an experimental refutation of the ideas of Nietzsche?"

On its first appearance the *Asrar-i-Khudi* took by storm the younger generation of Indian Muslim. "Iqbal," wrote one of them, "has come amongst us as a Messiah and has stirred the dead with life." If remains to be seen in what direction the awakened one will march. Will they be satisfied with a glorious but distant vision of the City of God, or will they adapt the new doctrine to other ends than those which its author has in view? Notwithstanding that he explicitly denounces the idea of nationalism, his admirers are already protesting that he does not mean what he says.

How far the influence of his work may ultimately go I will not attempt to prophesy. It has been said of him that "has is a man of his age and a man in advance of his age; he is also a man in disagreement with his age." We cannot regard his ideas as typical of any section of his co-religionists. They involve a radical change in the Muslim mind, and their real importance is not to be measured by the fact that such a change is unlikely to occur within a calculable time.

PROLOGUE

WHEN the world-illuming sun rushed upon Night
   like a brigand,
My weeping bedewed the face of the rose.
My tears washed away sleep from the eye
   of the narcissus,
My passion wakened the grass and made it grow.
The Gardener tried the power of my song, **(5)**
He sowed my verse and reaped a sword.
In the soil he planted only the seed of my tears.
And wove my lament with the garden, as
   warp and woof.
Tho' I am but a mote, the radiant sun is mine:
Within my bosom are a hundred dawns. **(10)**
My dust is brighter than Jamshîd's cup.[1]

---

1. *Jamshîd*, one of the mythical persian kings, is said to have possessed
a marvellous cup in which the whole world was displayed to him.

It knows things that are yet unborn in the world.

My thought hunted down and slung from the
    saddle a deer.

That has not yet leaped forth from the covert of
    non-existence.

Fair is my garden ere yet the leaves are green: **(15)**

Unborn roses are hidden in the skirt of my garment.

I struck dumb the musicians where they were
    gathered together,

I smote the heart-string of the universe,

Because the lute of my genius hath a rare melody:

Even to comrades my song is strange. **(20)**

I am born in the world as a new sun,

I have not learned the ways and fashions of the sky:

Not yet have the stars fled before my splendour,

Not yet is my quicksilver astir;

Untouched is the sea by my dancing rays, **(25)**

Untouched are the mountains by my crimson hue.

The eye of existence is not familiar with me;

I rise trembling, afraid to show myself.

From the East my dawn arrived and routed Night,

A fresh dew settled on the rose of the world. **(30)**

I am waiting for the votaries that rise at dawn;

Oh, happy they who shall worship my fire!

I have no need of the ear of Today,

I am the voice of the poet of Tomorrow

My own age does not understand my
    deep meanings.   **(35)**

My Joseph is not for this market.

I despair of my old companions.

My Sinai burns forsake of the Moses who is coming.

Their sea is silent, like dew,

But my dew is storm-ridden, like the ocean.   **(40)**

My song is of another world than theirs:

This bell calls other travellers to take the road,

Many a poet was born after his death,

Opened our eyes when his own were closed,

And journeyed forth again from nothingness.   **(45)**

Like roses blossoming o'er the earth of his grave.

Albeit caravans have passed through this desert.

They passed, as a camel steps, with little sound.

But I am a lover: loud crying is my faith:

The clamour of Judgement Day is one of
    my minions.   **(50)**

My song exceeds the range of the chord,

Yet I do not fear that my lute will break.

'Twere better for the waterdrop not to know my
   torrent,

Whose fury should rather madden the sea.

No river will contain my Oman:[2]   **(55)**

My flood requires whole seas to hold it.

Unless the bud expand into a bed of roses,

It is unworthy of my spring-cloud's bounty.

Lightnings slumber within my soul,

I sweep over mountain and plain.   **(60)**

Wrestle with my sea, if thou art a plain;

Receive my lightning if thou art a Sinai.

The Fountain of Life hath been given me to drink.

I have been made an adept of the mystery of Life.

The speck of dust was vitalised by my
   burning song: **(65)**

It unfolded wings and became a firefly.

No one hath told the secret which I will tell

Or threaded a pearl of thought like mine

---

2. The Sea of Omān is a (name given by the Arabs to the Persian Gulf.)

Come, if thou would'st know the secret of
    everlasting life!

Come, if thou would'st win both earth
    and heaven! **(70)**

Heaven taught me this lore,

I cannot hide it from comrades.

O Saki! arise and pour wine into the cup,!

Clear the vexation of Time from my heart!

The sparkling liquor that flows from Zemzen.[3] **(75)**

Were a beggar to worship it, he would become a king.

It makes thought more sober and wise,

It makes the keen eye keener,

It gives to a straw the weight of a mountain,

And to foxes the strength of lions. **(80)**

It causes dust to soar to the Pleiades

And a drop of waters well to the breadth of the sea.

It turns silence into the din of Judgement Day,

It makes the foot of the partridge red with blood of
    the hawk.

Arise and pour pure wine into my cup, **(85)**

---

3. The holy well at Makkah.

Pour moonbeams into the dark night of my thought,

That I may lead home the wanderer

And imbue the idle looker-on-with restless impatience;

And advance hotly on a new quest

And become known as the champion of a
      new spirit: **(90)**

And be to people of insight as the pupil to the eye,

And sink into the ear of the world, like a voice;

And exalt the worth of Poesy

And sprinkle the dry herbs with my tears.[4]

Inspired by the genius of the Master of Rum.[5]   **(95)**

I rehearse the sealed book of secretlore.

His soul is the flaming furnace,

I am but as the spark that gleams for a moment.

His burning candle consumed me, the moth;

His wine overwhelmed my goblet.   **(100)**

The master of Rum transmuted my earth to gold

---

4. *Iqbal* means to say that he will raise the value of his poetry by putting his deepest aspirations into it. The metaphor refers to the practice of herb-sellers who sprinkle water on their herbs in order to make them heavier and fetch more money.

5. *Jalālu'ddin Rûmî*, the greatest mystical poet of Persia (A.D. 1207-11 73). Most of his life was passed at Iconium in Galatia, for which reason he is generally known as "Rûmi, i.e., "The Anatolian."

And set my ashes aflame.

The grain of sand set forth from the desert,

That it might win the radiance of the sun.

I am a wave and I will come to rest in his sea, **(105)**

That I may make the glistening pearl mine own.

I who am drunken with the wine of his song.

Draw life from the breath of his words,

'Twas night: my heart would fain lament.

The silence was filled with my cries to God. **(110)**

I was complaining of the sorrows of the world.

And bewailing the emptiness of my cup.

At last mine eye could endure no more,

Broken with fatigue it went to sleep.

There appeared the Master, formed in the
   mould of Truth, **(115)**

Who wrote the Qur'ān in Persian.[6]

He said, "O frenzied lover,

Take a draught of love's pure wine.

Strike the chords of thine heart and rouse a tumultuous
   strain.

---

6. This refers to the famous *Masnavi of Jalālu'ddin Rûmî.*

Dash thine head against the goblet and thine eye
     against the lancet!   **(120)**

Make thy laughter the source of a hundred sighs.

Make the hearts of men bleed with thy tears!

How long wilt thou be silent, like a bud?

Sell thy fragrance cheep, like the rose!

Tongue-tied, thou art in pain: **(125)**

Cast thyself upon the fire, like rue![7]

Like the bell, breaks silence at last, and
     from every limb.

Utter forth a lamentation!

Thou art fire : fill the world with thy glow!

Make others burn with thy burning!

Proclaim the secrets of the old wine-seller;[8]

Be thou a surge of wine, and the crystal cup thy robe!

Shatter the mirror of fear,

Break the bottles in the bazaar!

Like the reed-flute, bring a message
     from the reed-bed;   **(135)**

---

7. Rue-seed, which is burned for the purpose of fumiation, crackles in
the fire.

8. "Wine" signifies the mysteris of divine love.

Give to Majnûn a message from the tribe of Laila![9]

Create a new style for thy song,

Enrich the assembly with thy piercing strains!

Up, and reinspire every living soul!

Say 'Arise!' and by that word quicken
    the living!   **(140)**

Up, and set thy feet on another path;

Put aside the passionate melancholy of old!

Become familiar with the delight of singing;

O bell of the caravan, awake!"

At these words my bosom was enkindled   **(145)**

And swelled with emotion like the flute;

I rose like music from the string

To prepare a Paradise for the ear.

I unveiled the mystery of the Self

And disclosed its wondrous secret   **(150)**

My being was an unfinished statue,

Uncomely, worthless, good for nothing.

Love chiselled me: I became a man.

And gained knowledge of the nature of the universe.

---

9. Majnûn is the Orlando Furioso of Arabia.

I have seen the movement of the sinews of the sky.

And the blood coursing in the veins of the moon.

Many a night I wept for Man's sake

That I might tear the veil from Life's mysteries.

And extract the secret of Life's constitution

From the laboratory of phenomena.   **(160)**

I who give beauty to his night, like the moon,

Am as dust in devotion to the pure Faith (Islam)—

A Faith renowned in hill and dale.

Which kindles in men's hearts a flame of
    undying song:

It sowed an atom and reaped a sun,   **(165)**

It harvested a hundred poets like Rûmî and Attar.

I am a sigh: I will mount to the heavens;

I am but smoke, yet am I sprung of fire.

Driven onward by high thoughts, my pen

Cast abroad the secret behind this veil,   **(170)**

That the drop may become co-equal with the sea

And the grain of sand grow into a Sahara.

Poetising is not the aim of this *masnavi*.

Beauty-worshipping and love-making is not its aim.

Persian

I am of India: Persian is not my native
      tongue;   **175**

I am like the crescent moon: my cup is not full.

Do not seek from me charm of style in exposition.

Do not seek not from me Khãnsãr and Isfahãn.[10]

Although the language of Hind is sweet as sugar,

Yet sweeter is the fashion of Persian speech.

My mind was enchanted by its loveliness.

My pen became as a twig of the Burning Bush.

Because of the loftiness of my thoughts,

Persian alone is suitable to them.

O Reader! do not find fault with the wine-cup.

But consider attentively the taste of the wine.

---

10. Khãnsãr, which lies about a hundred miles north-west of Isfahãn, was the birth-place of several Persian poets.

Solipsism Syndrome

1

SHOWING THAT THE SYSTEM OF THE UNIVERSE ORIGINATES IN THE SELF, AND THAT THE CONTINUATION OF THE LIFE OF ALL INDIVIDUALS DEPEND ON STRENGTHENING THE SELF.

THE form of existence is an effect of the Self,

Whatsoever thou seest is a secret of the Self,

When the Self awoke to consciousness.

It revealed the universe of Thought.

A hundred words are hidden in its essence: **(190)**

Self-affirmation brings Not-self to light.

By the Self the seed of opposition is sown in the word:

It imagines itself to be other than itself.

It makes from itself the forms of others   **(195)**

In order to multiply the pleasure of strife.

It is slaying by the strength of its arm

That it may become conscious of its own strength.

self-deceptions

Its self-deceptions are the essence of Life;

Like the rose, it lives by bathing itself
in blood.   **(200)**

For the sake of a single rose it destroys a hundred
rose gardens

And makes a hundred lamentation in quest of a single
melody.

For one sky it produces a hundred new moons,

And for one word a hundred discourses.

The excuse for this wastefulness and cruelty   **(205)**

Is the shaping and perfecting of spiritual beauty.

The loveliness of Shirin justifies the anguish of
Farhad.[1]

One fragrant navel justifies a hundred musk-deer.

'Tis the fate of moths to consume in flame:

The suffering of moths is justified by
the candle.   depicted   **(210)**

The pencil of the Self limned a hundred todays.

In order to achieve the dawn of a single morrow.

---

1. *Shirin* was loved by the Persian Emperor Khusrau Parwîz, *Farhâd*
fell in love with her and cast himself down a precipiece on hearing a
false rumour of her death.

Its flames burned a hundred Abrahams[2]

That the lamp of one Muhammad might be lighted.

Subject, object, means, and causes—   **(215)**

All these are forms which it assumes for the purpose
of action.

The Self rises, kindles, falls, glows, breathes,

Burns, shines, walks, and flies.

The spaciousness of Time is its arena.

Heaven is a billow of the dust on the road.   **(220)**

From its rose-planting the world abounds in roses;

Night is born of its sleep, day springs from its waking.

It divided its flame into sparks

And taught the understanding to worship particulars.

It dissolved itself and created the atoms   **(225)**

It was scattered for a little while and created sands.

Then it wearied of dispersion

And by re-uniting itself it became the mountains.

'Tis the nature of the Self to manifest itself:

In every atom slumbers the might of the Self.   **(230)**

Power that is expressed and inert

---

2. Abraham is said to have been cast on a burning pile by order of
Nimrod and miraculously preserved from harm.

Chains the faculties which lead to action.

Inasmuch as the life of the universe comes from the
power of the Self.

Life is in proportion to this power.

When a drop of water gets of Self's lesson
    by heart,   **(235)**

It makes its worthless existence a pearl.

Wine is formless because its self is weak;

It receives a form by favour of the cup.

Although the cup of wine assumes a form,

It is indebted to us for its motion.   **(240)**

When the mountain loses its self, it turns into sands

And complains that the sea surges over it;

The wave, so long as it remains a wave in the sea's
    bosom.[3]

Makes itself rider on the sea's back.

Light transformed itself into an eye   **(245)**

And moved to and fro in search of beauty;

When the grass found a means of growth in its self,

Its aspiration clove the breast of the garden.

The candle too concatenated itself

---

3. *I.e.*, so long as it remains as distinct individuals.

And built itself out of atoms: **(250)**

Then it made a practice of melting itself away and
fled from its self

Until at last it trickled down from its own eye, like
tears. *rim that fastens a jewel*

If the bezel had been more self secure by nature,

It would not have suffered wounds,

But since it derives its value from the
superscription, **(255)**

Its shoulder is galled by the burden of another's name.

Because the earth is firmly based on itself,

The captive moon goes round it perpetually.

The being of the sun is stronger than that of the earth:

Therefore is the earth fascinated by the sun's eye. **(260)**

The glory of the red beech fixes our gaze.

The mountains are enriched by its majesty:

Its raiment is woven of fire,

Its origin is one self-assertive seed.

When Life gathers strength from the Self, **(265)**

The river of Life expands into an ocean.

2

SHOWING THAT THE LIFE OF THE SELF COMES FROM FORMING DESIRES AND BRINGING THEM TO BIRTH.

LIFE is preserved by purpose:

Because of the goal its caravan-bell tinkles.

Life is latent in seeking.

Its origin is hidden in desire. (270)

Keep desire alive in thy heart,

Lest thy little dust become a tomb.

Desire is the soul of this world of hue and scent,

The nature of everything is a store-house of desire.

Desire sets the heart dancing in the breast. (275)

And by its glow the breast is made bright as a mirror.

It gives to earth the power of soaring.

It is a Khizr to the Moses of perception.[1]

---

1. *Cf.* Qur'ān ch. 18. v. 64-80. Khizr represents the mystic seer whose actions are misjudged by persons of less insight.

From the flame of desire the heart takes life,

And when it takes life, all dies that is not true. **(280)**

When it refrains from forming desires,

Its opinion breaks and it cannot soar.

Desire keeps the Self in perpetual uproar.

It is a restless wave of the Self's sea.

Desire is a noose for hunting ideals,   **(285)**

A binder of the book of deeds.

Negation of desire is death to the living,

Even as absence of heat extinguished the flame.

What is the source of our wakeful eye?

Our delight in seeing hath taken visible shape. **(290)**

The partridge's leg is derived from the elegance
        of its gait,

The nightingale's beak from its endeavour to sing.

Away from the seed-bed, the reed became happy:

The music was released from its prison.[2]

What is the essence of the mind that strives after new
        discoveries and scales the heavens?   **(295)**

Knowest thou what works this miracle?

---

2. *I.e.*, the reed was made into a flute.

'Tis desire that enriches Life,

And the mind is a child of its womb.

What are social organisation, customs and laws?

What is the secret of the novelties of science? **(300)**

A desire which realised itself by its own strength

And burst forth from the heart and took shape.

Nose, hand, brain, eye, and ear,

Though, imagination, feeling, memory, and understanding—

All these are weapons devised by Life for self-preservation   **(305)**

In its ceaseless struggle,

The object of science and art is not knowledge,

The object of the garden is not the bud and the flower.

Science is an instrument for the preservation of Life.

Science is a means of invigorating the Self.   **(310)**

Science and art are servants of Life,

Slaves born and bred in its house,

Rise, O thou who art strange to Life's mystery,

Rise intoxicated with the wine of an ideal,   **(315)**

An ideal shining as the dawn,

A blazing fire to all that is other than God,

An ideal higher than Heaven—

Winning, captivating, enchanting men's hearts;

A destroyer of ancient falsehood,

Fraught with turmoil, and embodiment of
    the Last Day.

We live by forming ideals,   **(320)**

We glow with the sunbeams of desire!

3

SHOWING THAT THE SELF IS STRENGTHENED BY LOVE.[1]

THE luminous point whose name is the Self

Is the life-spark beneath our dust.

By Love it is made more lasting, **(325)**

More living, more burning, more glowing.

From Love proceeds the radiance of its being.

And the development of its unknown possibilities.

Its nature gathers fire from Love,

Love instructs it to illumine the world. **(330)**

Love fears neither sword nor dagger,

Love is not born of water and air and earth.

Love makes peace and war in the world,

Love is the Fountain of Life, Love is the flashing
sword of Death.

---

1. For the sense which Iqbal attaches to the word "love," see the
Introductions, p. xxv.

The hardest rocks are shivered by Love's glance: **(335)**

Love of God at last becomes wholly God,

Learn thou to love, and seek a beloved:

Seek an eye like Noah's, a heart like Job's!

Transmute thy handful of earth into gold,

Kiss the threshold of a Perfect Man![2]   **(340)**

Like Rumî, light the candle

And burn Rum in the fire of Tabriz![3]

There is a beloved hidden within thine heart:

I will show him to thee, if thou hast eye to see.

His lovers are fairer than the fair,   **(345)**

Sweeter and comelier and more beloved.

By love of him the heart is made strong

And earth rubs shoulders with the Pleiades.

The soil of Najd was quickened by his grace

And fell into a rapture and rose to the skies.[4] **(350)**

In the Muslim's heart is the home of Muhammad,

---

2. A Prophet or saint.

3. See note on line 95, Tabriz is an allusion to Shams-i-Tabriz the spiritual director of *Jalālu'ddin Rûmî*.

4. Najd, the Highlands of Arabia, is celebrated in love-romance. I need only mention Lailā and Majnûn.

All our glory is from the name of Muhammad.

Sinai is but an eddy of the dust of his house,

His dwelling-place is a sanctuary to the Ka'ba Itself.

Eternity is less than a moment of his time,   **(355)**

Eternity receives increase from his essence.

He slept on a mat of rushes,

But the crown of Chosroes was under his people's feet.

He chose the nightly solitude of Mount Hira,

And he founded a state and laws and
  government.   **(360)**

He passed many a night with sleepless eyes

In order that the Muslims might sleep on the throne
  of Persia.

In the hour of battle, iron was melted by the flash of
  his sword;

In the hour of prayer, tears fell like rain from his eye.

When he prayed for Divine help, his sword
  answered "Amen"   **(365)**

And extirpated the race of kings.

He instituted new laws in the world,

He brought the empires of antiquity to an end.

With the key of religion he opened the door of this world:

The womb of the world never bore his like.   **(370)**

In his sight high and low were one,

He sat with his slave at one table.

The daughter of the chieftain of Tai was taken prisoner
    in battle[5]

And brought into the exalted presence;

Her feet in chains, unveiled,   **(375)**

And her neck bowed with shame

When the Prophet saw that the poor girl had no veil,

He covered her face with his own mantle.

We are more naked than that lady of Taj,

We are unveiled before the nations of the world. **(380)**

In him is our trust on the Day of Judgement,

And in this world too he is our protector.

Both his favour and his wrath are entirely a mercy:

That is a mercy to his friends and this to his foes.

He opened the gate of mercy to his enemies,   **(385)**

He gave to Makkah the message, "No penalty shall
    be laid upon you."

He who know not the bonds of country

---

5. Her father Hātim of Tai, is proverbial in the East for his hospitality.

Resemble sight, which is one though it be the light of
    two eyes.

We belong to the Hijaz and China and Persia,

Yet we are the dew of one smiling dawn.   **(390)**

We are all under the spell of the eye of the cup bearer
    from Makkah.

We are united as wine and cup.

He burnt clean away distinction of lineage.

His fire consumed this trash and rubble.

We are like a rose with many petals but with one
    perfume: **(395)**

He is the soul of this society, and he is one

We are the secret concealed in his heart:

He speak out fearlessly, and we were revealed.

The song of love for him fills my silent reed,

A hundred notes throb in my bosom.   **(400)**

How shall I tell what devotion he inspires?

A block of dry wood wept at parting from him.[6]

The Muslim's being is where the manifests his glory:

Many a Sinai springs from the dust on his path.

---

6. The story of the pulpit that wept when Muhammad descended from
it occurs, I think, in the *Masnavî.*

My image was created by his mirror,   **(405)**

My dawn rises from the sun of his breast.

My repose is a perpetual fever,

My evening hotter than the morning of
    Judgement Day:[7]

He is the April cloud and I his garden,

My vine is bedewed with his rain.   **(410)**

I sowed mine eye in the field of Love

And reaped a harvest of vision.

"The soil of Madinah is sweeter than both worlds:

Oh, happy the town where dwell the Beloved![8]

I am lost in admiration of the style of
    Mulla Jami: **(415)**

His verse and prose are a remedy for my immaturity.

He has written poetry overflowing with beautiful ideas

And has threaded pearls in praise of the Master—

"Muhammad is the preface to the book of the universe;

All the worlds are slaves and he is the Master." **(420)**

From the wine of Love spring many spiritual qualities:

Amongst the attributes of Love is blind devotion.

The saint of Bistam, who in devotion was unique,

---

7. When, according to Muhammadans belief, the sun will rise
in the west.

8. A quotation from the Masnavî. The Prophet was buried at Madinah.

Abstained from eating a water-melon.[9]

Be a lover constant in devotion to thy beloved, **(425)**

That thou mayst cast thy nose and capture God.

Sojourn for a while on the Hira of the heart.[10]

Abandon self and the flee to God.

Strengthened by God, return to thy self

And break the heads of the Lat and
     Uzzā of sensuality[11]   **(430)**

By the might of Love evoke an army

Reveal thyself on the Farān of Love,[12]

That the Lord of the Ka'ba may show thee favour

And make thee the object of the text, "Lo, I will
     appoint a vicegerent on the earth."[13]

---

9. *Bāyazîd* of Bistān died in A.D. 875. He refused to eat a water-melon, saying he had no assurance that the Prophet had even tested that fruit.

10. Muhammad used to retire to a cave on Mount Hirā, near Makkah, for purpose of solitary meditation.

11. *Lāt* and *Uzzā* were goddesses worshipped by the heathen Arabs.

12. *Farān*, name of a mountain in the neighbourhood of Makkah.

13. Qur'ān, ch. 2, v. 28. In these words, which were addressed to the angels, God foretold the creation of Adam.

4

SHOWING THAT THE SELF IS WEAKENED BY ASKING

O THOU who hast gathered taxes from lions, **(435)**

They need hath caused thee to become a fox in disposition.

Thy maladies are the result of indigence:

This disease is the source of thy pain.

It is robbing thine high thoughts of their dignity.

And putting out the light of thy noble imagination. **(440)**

Quaff rosy wine from the jar of existence!

Snatch thy money from the purse of Time!

Like Omar, come down from thy camel![1]

Beware of incurring obligations, beware!

How long wilt thou sue for office **(445)**

---

1. This alludes to a story told of the Caliph Omar, who while riding a camel dropped his whip and insisted on dismounting in order to pick it up himself.

new simile

And ride like children on a reed?
A nature that fixes is glaze on the sky
Becomes debased by receiving benefits.
By asking, poverty is made more abject;
By begging, the beggar is made poorer,   **(450)**
Asking disintegrates the Self
And deprives of illumination the Sinai-bush
    of the Self.
Do not scatter thy handful of dust;
Like the moon, scrape food from thine own side!   ✳
Albeit thou art poor and wretched   **(455)**
And overwhelmed by affliction,
Seek not thy daily bread from the bounty of another,
Seek not water from the fountain of the sun,
Lest thou be put to shame before the Prophet
On the Day when every soul shall be
    stricken with fear.   **(460)**
The moon gets sustenance from the table of the sun
And bears the brand of his bounty on her heart.
Pray God for courage! Wrestle with Fortune!
Do not sully the honour of the pure religion!
He who swept the rubbish of idols out
    of the Ka'ba   **(465)**
Said that God loves a man that earns his living

Woe to him that accepts bounty from another's table

And lets his neck be bent with benefits!

He hath consumed himself with the lightning of the
    favours bestowed on him,

He hath sold his honour for a paltry coin,   **(470)**

Happy the man who thirsting in the sun

Does not crave of Khizr a cup of water![2]

His brow is not moist with the shame of beggary;

He is a man still, not a piece of clay,

That noble youth walks under heaven   **(475)**

With his head erect like the pine.

Are his hands empty? The more is he master of
    himself.

Do his fortunes languish? The more alert is he.

A whole ocean, if gained by begging is but a sea of
    fire;

Sweet is a little dew gathered by one's own hand. **(480)**

Be a man of honour, and like the bubble.

 Keep the cup inverted even in the midst of the sea![3]

---

2. Khizr is supposed to have drunk of the Fountain of Life.

3. The bubble is compared to an inverted cup, which of course received
nothing.

5

SHOWING THAT WHEN THE SELF IS STRENGTHENED BY LOVE IT GAINS DOMINION OVER THE OUTWARD AND INWARD FORCES OF THE UNIVERSE

WHEN the Self is made strong by Love

Its power rules the whole world.

The Heavenly Sage who adorned the

   sky with stars   **(485)**

Plucked these buds from the bough of the Self.

Its hand becomes God's hand,

The moon is split by its fingers.[1]

It is the arbitrator in all the quarrels of the world.

Its command is obeyed by Darius and Jamshid. **(490)**

I will tell thee a story of Bu Ali,[2]

---

1. Alluding to a well-known miracle of the Prophet (Qur'ān, ch. 54, v. 1)

2. Sheikh Sharafu'ddin of Pānipat, who is better known as Bu Ali Qalandar, was a great saint. He died about A.D. 1325.

Whose name is renowned in India,

Him who sang of the ancient rose-garden

And discoursed to us about the lovely rose:

The air of his fluttering skirt   **(495)**

Made a Paradise of this fire-born country.

His young disciple went one day to the bazaar—

The wine of Bu Ali's discourse had turned his head.

The governor of the city was coming along on
    horseback,

His servant and staff-bearer rode beside him.   **(500)**

The forerunner shouted, "O senseless one,

Do not get in the way of the governor's escort!"

But the dervish walked on with drooping head.

Sunk in the sea of his own thoughts.

The staff-bearer, drunken with pride,   **(505)**

Broken his staff on the head of the dervish.

Who stepped painfully out of the governor's way.

Sad and sorry, with a heavy heart.

He came to Bu Ali and complained

And released the tears from his eyes.   **(510)**

Like lightning that falls on mountains,

The Sheikh poured forth a fiery torrent of speech.

He let loose from his soul a strange fire,

He gave an order to his secretary:

"Take thy pen and write a letter **(515)**

From a dervish to a sultan!

Say, 'Thy governor has broken my servant's head;

He has cast burning coals on his own life.

Arrest this wicked governor,

Or else I will bestow thy kingdom on another"**(520)**

The letter of the saint who had access to God

Caused the monarch to tremble in every limb.

His body was filled with aches,

He grew as pale as the evening sun.

He sought out a handcuff for the governor **(525)**

And entreated Bu Ali to pardon this offence.

Khusrau, the sweet-voiced eloquent poet.[3]

Whose harmonies flow from the creative mind

And whose genius hath the soft brilliance of
   moonlight,

---

3. Amir Khusrau of Delhi, the most celebrated of the Persian poets of India.

Was chosen to be the king's ambassador.   **(530)**

When he entered Bu Ali's presence and
    played his lute,

His song melted the fakir's soul like glass.

One strain of poesy bought the grace

Of a kingdom that was firm as a mountain.

Do not wound the hearts of dervishes,   **(535)**

Do not throw thyself into burning fire!

6

A TALE OF WHICH THE MORAL IS THAT NEGATION OF THE SELF IS A DOCTRINE INVENTED BY THE SUBJECT RACES OF MANKIND IN ORDER THAT BY THIS MEANS THEY MAY SAP AND WEAKEN THE CHARACTER OF THEIR RULERS

HAST thou heard that in the time of old

The sheep dwelling in a certain pasture

So increased and multiplied

That they feared no enemy?

At last, from the malice of Fate,

Their breasts were smitten by a shaft of calamity.

The tigers sprang forth from the jungle

And rushed upon the sheepfold.

Conquest and dominion are sings of strength, *things*

Victory is the manifestation of strength.

Those fierce tigers beat the drum of sovereignty,

They deprived the sheep of freedom.

For as much as tigers must have their prey,

That meadow was crimsoned with the
　　blood of the sheep.   **(550)**

One of the sheep which was clever and acute.

Old in years, cunning was a weather-beaten wolf,

Being grieved at the fate of his fellows

And sorely vexed by the violence of the tigers,

Made complaint of the course of Destiny   **(555)**

And sought by craft to restore the fortunes of his race.

The weak, in order to preserve themselves.

Seek device from skilled intelligence.

In slavery, for the sake of repelling harm,

The power of scheming becomes quickened.   **(560)**

And when the madness of revenge gains hold,

The mind of the slave meditates rebellion.

"Ours is a hard knot," said this sheep to himself,

"The ocean of our griefs hath no shore,

By force we sheep cannot escape
　　from the tiger: **(565)**

Our legs are silver, his paws are steel.

'Tis not possible, however much one exhorts
　　and counsels.

So much for apostles

To create in a sheep the disposition of a wolf.

But to make the furious tiger a sheep—that is possible:

To make him unmindful of his nature—
    that is possible." **(570)**

He became as a Prophet inspired,

And began to preach to the blood-thirsty tigers.

He cried out, "O ye insolent liars,

Who wot not of a day of ill luck that shall continue
    for ever![1]

I am possessed of spiritual power, **(575)**

I am an apostle sent by God for the tigers.

I come as a light for the eye that is dark,

I come to establish laws and give commandments.

Repent of your blameworthy deeds;

O plotters of evil, bethink yourselves
    of good! **(580)**

Whoso is violent and strong is miserable:

Life's solidity depends on self-denial.

The spirit of the righteous is fed by fodder:

The vegetarian is pleasing unto God,

The sharpness of your teeth brings disgrace
    upon you **(585)**

---

1. These expressions are borrowed from the Qur'ān.

And makes the eye of your perception blind.

christ

Paradise is for the weak alone,

Strength is but a means to perdition.

It is wicked to seek greatness and glory,

Penury is sweeter than princedom.   **(590)**

Lightning does not threaten the corn-seed:

If the seed become a stack, it is unwise.

If you are sensible, you will be a mote of sand,
    not a Sahara,

So that you may enjoy the sunbeams.

O thou that delightest in the slaughter of sheep **(595)**

Slay thy self, and thou wilt have honour!

Life is rendered unstable

By violence, oppression, revenge and exercise of
    power.

Though trodden underfoot, the grass grows up time
    after time

And washes the sleep of death from its eye again and
    again   **(600)**

Forget thy self, if thou art wise!

If thou dost not forget thy self, thou art mad.

nursery tale

Close thine eyes, close thine ears, close thy lips,[2]

That thy thought may reach the lofty sky!"

This pasturage of the world is naught, naught: **(605)**

O fool, do not torment thyself for a phantom!

The tiger-tribe was exhausted by hard struggles,

They had set their hearts on enjoyment of luxury.

This soporific advice pleased them,

In their stupidity they swallowed the charm
    of the sheep. **(610)**

He that used to make sheep his prey

Now embraced a sheep's religion.

The tigers took kindly to a diet of fodder:

At length their tigerish nature was broken.

The fodder blunted their teeth **(615)**

And put out the awful fleshings of their eyes.

By degrees courage ebbed from their breasts.

The sheen departed from mirror.

That frenzy of uttermost exertion remained not.

That craving after action dwelt in their
    hearts no more. **(620)**

---

2. Quoted from the _Masnavî_.

They lost the power of ruling and the resolution to be
 independent,

They lost reputation, prestige and for-turn. _fortune_

Their paws that were as iron became strengthless;

Their souls died and their bodies became tombs.

Bodily strength diminished while spiritual fear
 increased: (625)

Spiritual fear robbed them of courage.

Lack of courage produced a hundred diseases—

Poverty, pusillanimity, low mindedness.

The wakeful tiger was lulled to slumber by the
 sheep's charm:

He called his decline Moral Culture.   (630)

7

TO THE EFFECT THAT PLATO, WHOSE THOUGHT HAS DEEPLY INFLUENCED THE MYSTICISM AND LITERATURE OF ISLAM, FOLLOWED THE SHEEP'S DOCTRINE, AND THAT WE MUST BE ON OUR GUARD AGAINST HIS THEORIES.[1]

PLATO, the prime ascetic and sage.

Was one of that ancient flock of sheep.

His Pegasus went astray in the darkness of idealism

And dropped its shoe amidst the rocks of actuality.

He was so fascinated by the invisible   **635**

---

1. The direct influence of Platonism on Muslim thought has been comparatively slight. When the Muslims began to study Greek philosophy, thy turned to Aristotle. The genuine writings of Aristotle, however, were not accessible to them. They studied translations of books passing under his name, which were the work of Neoplatonists, so that what they believed to be Aristotelian doctrine was in fact the philosopy of Platinus, Proelus, and the later Neoplatonic school. Indirectly, therefore, Plato has profoundly influenced the intellectual and spiritual development of Islam and may be called, if not the father of Muhammadan mysticism, at any rate its presiding genius.

Platinus, Proelus

That he made hand, eye, and ear of no account.

"To die," said, he, "is the secret of Life:

The candle is glorified by being put out."

He dominates our thinking,

His cup sends us to sleep and takes the sensible
     world away from us.   **640**

He is a sheep in man's clothing,

The soul of the Sufi bows to his authority.

He soared with his intellect to the highest heaven

And called the world of phenomena a myth.

'Twas his work to dissolve the structure
     of Life   **645**

And cut the bough of Life's fair tree asunder.

The thought of Plato regarded loss as profit,

His philosophy declared that being is not-being.

He natures drowsed and created a dream

His mind's eye created a mirage.   **650**

Since he was without any taste for action

His soul was enraptured by the non-existent.

He disbelieved in the material universe

And became the creator of invisible Ideas.

Sweet is the world of phenomena to be living spirit,

Dear is the world of Ideas to the dead spirit:

Its gazelles have no grave of movement,

Its partridges are denied the pleasure of walking
 daintily.

Its dewdrops are unable to quiver,

Its birds have no breadth in their breasts, **660**

Its seed does not desire to grow,

Its moths do not know how to flutter.

Our recluse had no remedy but flight:

He could not endure the noise of this world.

He set his heart on the glow of a
 quenched flame **665**

And depicted a word steeped in opium.

He spread his wings towards the sky

And never came down to his nest again.

His phantasy is sunk in the jar of heaven:

I know not whether it is the dregs or the brick of the
 wine-jar[2] **670**

The peoples were poisoned by his intoxication:

He slumbered and took no delight in deeds.

---

2. *I.e.*, it is worthless anyhow. In the East a brick is placed beneath or
over the wine-jar. Some Muslim writers confuse Plato with Diogenes
the Cynic, who is said to have lived in a cask.

8

CONCERNING THE TRUE NATURE OF POETRY AND REFORM OF ISLAMIC LITERATURE

'TIS the brand of desire makes the blood of man run
    warm,

By the lamp of desire this dust is enkindled.

By desire Life's cup is brimmed with wine,   **675**

So that Life leaps to its feet and marches briskly on.

Life is occupied with conquest alone,

And the one charm for conquest is desire.

Life is the hunter and desire the snare,

Desire is Love's message to Beauty.   **680**

Wherefore doth desire swell continuously

The bass and treble of Life's song?

Whatsoever is good and fair and beautiful

Is our guide in the wilderness of seeking,

Its image becomes impressed on thine heart,   **685**

Desire / Poet

It creates desires in thine heart.

Beauty is the creator of desire's spring-tide,

Desire is nourished by the display of Beauty.

'Tis in the poet's breast that beauty unveils,

Poet

'Tis from his Sinai the Beauty's beams arise. **690**

By his look the fair is made fairer,

Through his enchantments Nature is more beloved.

From his lips the nightingale hath learned her song,

And his rouge hath brightened the cheek of the rose.

'Tis his passion burns in the heart of

the moth,   **695**

'Tis he that lends glowing hues to love-tales.

Sea and land are hidden within his water and clay.[1]

A hundred new words are concealed in his heart,

Ere tulips blossomed in his brain

There was heard on note of joy or grief.   **700**

His music breathes o'er us a wonderful enchantment,

His pen draws a mountain with a single hair.

His thoughts dwell with the moon and the stars,

He creates beauty and knows not what is ugly.

He is a Khizr, and amidst his darkness is the Fountain

---

1. *I.e.*, in his body.

of Life:[2]   **705**

All things that exist are made more living by his tears.

Heavily we go, like raw novices,

Stumbling on the way to the goal.

His nightingale hath played a tune

And laid a plot to beguile us.   **710**

That he may lead us into Life's Paradise,

And that Life's bow may become a full circle.

Caravans march at the sound of his bell

And follow the voice of his pipe;

When his zephyr blows in our garden,   **715**

It slowly steals into the tulips and roses.

His witchery makes Life develop itself

And become self-questioning and impatient.

He invites the whole world to his table;

He lavishes his fire as though it were
     cheap as air.   **720**

Woe to a people that resigns itself to death.

And whose poet turns away from the joy of living!

---

2. Khizr, according to the legend, discovered the Fountain of Life in
the Land of Darkness.

bad poet

bad poet

His mirror shows beauty as ugliness,

His honey leaves a hundred stings in the heart.

His kiss robs the rose of freshness,   **725**

He takes away from the nightingale's heart the
    joy of flying.

The sinews are relaxed by his opium,

Thou payest for his song with the life..

He bereaves the cypress of delight in its beauty.

His cold breath makes a pheasant of the
    male falcon.   **730**

He is a fish, and from the breast upward a man,

Like the Sirens in the ocean,

With his song he enchants the pilot

And casts the ship to the bottom of the sea.

His melodies steal firmness from thine heart,   **735**

His magic persuades thee that death is life.

He takes from thy soul the desire of existence,

He extracts from thy mine the blushing ruby.

He dresses gain in the garb of loss,

He makes everything praiseworthy blameful   **740**

He plunges thee in a sea of thought

bad poet

And makes thee a stranger to action.

He is sick, and by his words our sickness is increased:

The more his cup goes round, the more sick are they
    that quaff it.

There are no lightning-rains in his April,   745

His garden is a mirage of colour and perfume.

His beauty hath no dealings with Truth,

There are none but flawed pearls in his sea.

Slumber he deemed sweeter than waking:

Our fire was quenched by his breath.   750

By the chant of his nightingale the heart was poisoned:

Under his heap of roses lurked a snake.

Beware of his decanter and cup!

Beware of his sparkling wine!

O thou whom his wine hath laid low   755

And who look'st to his glass for thy rising dawn,

O thou whose heart hath been chilled by his melodies,

Thou hast drunk deadly poison through the ear!

Thy way of life is a proof of thy degeneracy,

The strings of thine instrument are
    out of tune,   760

'Tis pampered ease hath made thee so wretched,

It's

A disgrace to Islam throughout the world,

One can bind thee with the vein of a rose.

One can wound thee with a zephyr.

Love hath been put to shame by thy wailing,   **765**

His fair picture hath been fould by thy brush.

Thy illness hath paled his cheek,

The coldness hath taken the glow from his fire.

He is heartsick from thy heartsicknesses,

And enfeebled by thy feeblenesses.   **770**

His cup is full of childish tears,

His house is furnished with distressful sighs.[3]

He is a drunkard begging at tavern-doors.

Stealing glimpses of beauty from lattices,

Unhappy, melancholy, injured,   **775**

Kicked well-nigh to death by the warder;

Wasted like a reed by sorrows,

On his lips a store of complaints against Heaven.

Flattery and spite are the mettle of his mirror,

---

3. In this passage the author assails the Persian and Urdu poetry so much in favour with his contemporaries.

Helplessness his comrade of old;   **780**

A miserable base-born unkerling

Without worth or hope or object,

Whose lamentations have sucked the marrow from
(thy) soul

And driven off gentle sleep from thy neighbours' eyes.

Alas for a love whose fire is extinct,   **785**

A love that was born in the Holy Place and died in the
house of idols!

On, if thou hast the coin of poesy in thy purse,

Rub it on the touchstone of Life!

Clear-seeing thought shows the way to action,

As the lightning-flash precedes the thunder.   **790**

It behoves thee to meditate well concerning literature,

It behoves thee to go back to Arabia:

Thou must needs give thine heart to the Salma of
Arady,[4]

That the morn of the Hijaz may blossom from the night

---

4. Arabic odes usually began with a prelude in which the poet makes
mention of his beloved; and her name is often Salmā. Here "the Salmā
of Araby" refers to purely Muslim ideals in literature and religion.

'bad' Muslim
Iranian poets

of Kurdistan.[5]

Thou hast gathered roses from the garden
of Persia   **795**

And seen the springtide of India and Iran:

Now taste a little of the heat of the desert,

Drink the old wine of the date!

Lay thine head for once on it hot breast.

Yield thy body awhile to its scorching wind!   **800**

For a long time thou hast turned about on a bed of
silk:

Now accustom thyself to rough cotton!

For generations thou hast danced on tulips

And bathed thy cheek in dew, like the rose:

Now throw thy-self on the burning sand   **805**

---

5. It is related that an ignorant Kurd came to some students and besought them to instruct him in the mysteries of Sufism. They told him that he must fasten a rope to the roof of his house, then tie the loose end to his feet and suspend himself, head downwards; and that he must remain in this posture as long as possible, reciting continually some words of gibberish which they taught him. The poor man did not perceive that he was being mocked. He followed their instructions and passed the whole night repeating the words given him. God rewarded his faith, and sincerity by granting him illumination, so that he became a saint and could discourse, learnedly on the most abstruse matters of mystical theology. Afterwards he used to say, "In the evening I was Kurd, but the next morning I was an Arab."

unconvincing & rather silly
story + its racist

And plunge into the fountain of Zemzem!

How long wilt thou fain lament like the nightingale?

How long make thine abode in gardens?

O thou whose auspicious snare would do honour to
     the Phoenix,

Build a nest on the high mountains,   **810**

A nest embosomed in lightning and thunder,

Loftier than eagle's eyrie,

That thou mayst be fit for Life's battle,

That thy body and soul may burn in Life's fire!

9

SHOWING THAT THE EDUCATION OF THE SELF HAS THREE STAGES : OBEDIENCE, SELF-CONTROL, AND DIVINE VICEGERENCY

1. OBEDIENCE

SERVICE and toil are traits of the camel,   **815**

Patience and perseverance are ways of the camel.

Noiselessly he steps along the sandy track,

He is the ship of those who voyage in the desert.

Every thicket knows the print of his foot:

He eats seldom, sleeps little, and is inured
    to toil.   **820**

He carries rider, baggage, and litter:

He trots on and on to the journey's end,

Rejoicing in his speed,

More patient in travel than his rider,

Thou, too, do not refuse the burden of Duty: **825**

So wilt thou enjoy the best dwelling-place, which is
    with God.

Endeavour to obey, O heedless one!

Liberty is the fruit of compulsion.

By obedience the man of no worth is made worthy;

By disobedience his fire is turned to ashes.   830

Whoso would master the sun and stars,

Let him make himself a prisoner of Law!

The air becomes fragrant when it is imprisoned in the
    flower-bud;

The perfume become musk when it is confined in the
    navel of the musk-deer.

The star moves towards its goal   835

With head bowed in surrender to a law.

The grass springs up in obedience to the law of growth:

When it abandons that, it is trodden underfoot.

To burn unceasingly is the law of the tulip.

And so the blood leaps in its veins.   840

Drops of water become a sea by the law of union,

And grains of sand become a Sahara.

Since Law makes everything strong within,

Why dost thou neglect this source of strength?

O thou that art emancipated from the
old Custom.[1]   **845**

Adorn thy feet once more with the same
fine silver chain!

Do not complain of the hardness of the Law,

Do not transgress the statutes of Muhammad!

2. SELF-CONTROL

Thy soul cares only for itself, like the camel:

It is self-conceited, self-governed, and
self-willed.   **850**

Be a man, get its halter into thine hand,

That thou mayst become a pearl albeit thou
art a potter's vessel.

He that does not command himself

Becomes a receiver of commands from others.

When they moulded thee of clay,   **855**

Love and fear were mingled in thy making:

Fear of this world and of the world to come,
fear of death,

Fear of all the pains of earth and heaven;

1. The religious law of Islam.

Love of riches and power, love of country,

Love of self and kindred and wife.   **860**

Man, in whom clay is mixed with water, is
    fond of ease,

Devoted to wickedness and enamoured of evil.

Solongas thou hold'st the staff of "There is
    no god but He,"[2]

Thou wilt break every spell of fear.

One to whom God is as the soul in his body,   **865**

His neck is not bowed before vanity.

Fear finds no way into his bosom,

His heart is afraid of none but Allah.

Whoso dwells in the world of Negation.[3]

Is freed from the bonds of wife and child.   **870**

He withdraws his gaze from all except God

And lays the knife to the throat of his son.[4]

Though single, he is like a host in onset:

Life is cheaper in his eyes than wind.

---

2. The first article of the Mohammadan creed.

3. *I.e.*, denies every object of worship except Allah.

4. Like Abraham when he was about to sacrifice Isaace. or (as Muslims
generally believe) Ishmael.

The profession of Faith is the shell, and prayer is the
     pearl within it: **875**

The Muslim's heart deems prayer a lesser pilgrimage.[5]

In the Muslim's hand prayer is like a dagger.

Killing sin and forwardness and wrong.

Fasting makes an assault upon hunger and thirst.

And breaches the citadel of sensuality.   **880**

The pilgrimage enlightens the soul of the Faithful:

It teaches separation from one's home and destroys
     attachment to one's native land;

It is an act of devotion in which all feel themselves to
     be one,

It binds together the leaves of the book of religion,

Almsgiving causes love of riches to
     pass away   **885**

And makes equality familiar;

It fortifies the heart with righteousness,[6]

---

5. The lesser pilgrimage (*umra*) in not obligatory like the greater
pilgrimage (*hajj*).

6. The original quotes part of a verse in the Qur'ān (Ch. 3. v. 86), where
it is said, "Ye shall never attain unto righteousness until ye give in alms
of that which ye love."

greed

It increases wealth and diminishes fondness for wealth.

All this is a means of strengthening thee:

Thou art impregnable, if thy Islam be strong. **890**

Draw might from the litany "O Almighty One!"

That thou mayst ride the camel of thy body.[7]

3. DIVINE VICEGERENCY[8]

If thou canst rule thy camel, thou wilt rule the world.

And wear on thine head the crown of Solomon.

cheap temptation

Thou wilt be the glory of the world whilst the
    world lasts,   **895**

And thou wilt reign in the kingdom incorruptible.

'Tis sweet to be God's vicegerent in the world

And exercise sway over the elements.

God's vicegerent is as the soul of the universe,

His being is the shadow of the

---

7. *I.e.*, overcome the lusts of the flesh.

8. Here Iqbal interprets in his own way the Sûfi doctrine of the *Insãn al-kãmil* or Perfect Man, which teaches that every man is potentially a microcosm, and that when he has become spiritually perfect, all the Divine attributes are displayed by him, so that as saint of Prophet he is the God-man, the representative and vicegerent of God on earth.

Greatest Name.   **900**

He knows the mysteries of part and whole,

He executes the command of Allah in the world.

When he pitches his tent in the wide world.

He rolls up this ancient carpet.[9]

His genius abounds with life and desires to
    manifest itself: **905**

He will bring another world into existence.

A hundred words like this world of parts and wholes

Spring up, like roses, from the seed of his imagination.

He makes every raw nature ripe,

He puts the idols out of the sanctuary.   **910**

Heart-strings give forth music at his touch.

He wakes and sleeps for God alone.

He teaches age the melody of youth

And endows everything with the radiance of youth.

To the human race he brings both a glad message and
    a warning,   **915**

He comes both as a soldier and as a marshal and prince.

He is the final cause of "God taught Adam the names

---

9. *I.e.*, his appearance marks the end of an epoch.

of all things,"[10]

He is the inmost sense of "Glory to Him that
    transported His servant by night."[11]

His white hand is strengthened by the staff.[12]

His knowledge is twinned with the power of a
    perfect man.   920

When that bold cavalier seizes the reins,

The steed of Time gallops faster.

His awful men makes the Red Sea dry,

He leads Israel out of Egypt.

At his cry, "Arise," the dead spirits   925

Rise in their bodily tomb, like pines in the field.

His person is an atonement for all the world,

By his grandeur the world is saved.[13]

His protecting shadow makes the mote familiar with
    the sun,

His rich substance makes precious all

---

10. Qur'ān, ch. 2, v. 29. The Ideal Man is the final cause of creation.

11. Qur'ān, ch. 17, v. 1, referring to the Ascension on the Prophet.

12. For the white hand (of Moses) *of*, Qur'ān, ch. 7, v. 105, ch. 26, v.
32, and Exodus, ch. 4, v. 6.

13. These four lines may allude to Jesus, regarded as a type of the
Perfect Man.

The Perfect Man

that exists.   **930**

He bestows life by his miraculous actions,

He renovates old ways of life.

Splendid visions rise from the print of his foot.

Many a Moses is entranced by his Sinai.

He gives a new explanation of Life,   **935**

A new interpretation of this dream.

His hidden being is Life's mystery,

The unheard music of Life's harp.

Nature travels in blood for generations.

To compose the harmony of his personality.   **940**

Our handful of earth has reach the zenith,

For that champion will come forth from this dust!

There sleeps amidst the ashes of our To-day

The flame of a world-consuming morrow.

Our bad enfolds a garden of roses,   **945**

Our eyes are bright with To-morrows's dawn.

Appear, O rider of Destiny!

Appear, O light of the dark realm of Change!

Illumine the scene of existence.

Dwell in the blackness of our eyes!   **950**

Silence the noise of the nations,

Imparadise our ears with thy music!

Arise and tune the harp of brotherhood,

Give us back the cup of the wine of love!

Bring once more days of peace to the world,   **955**

Give a message of peace to them that seek battle!

Mankind are the cornfield and thou the harvest,

Thou art the goal of Life's caravan.

The leaves are scattered by Autumn's fury:

Oh, do thou pass over our gardens
    as the Spring!   **960**

Receive from our downcast brows

The homage of little children and of young
    men and old!

It is to thee that we owe our dignity

And silently undergo the pains of life.

Imparadise

10

SETTING FORTH THE INNER MEANINGS
OF THE NAMES OF ALI

ALI is the first Muslim and the King
of men,   965

In Love's eyes Ali is the treasure of the Faith.

Devotion to his family inspire we with life

So that I am as a shining pearl.

Like the narcissus, I am entraptured with gazing:

Like perfume, I am straying though his
pleasure-garden.   970

If holy water gushes from my earth, he is the source;

If wine pours from my grapes, he is the cause.

I am dust, but his sun hath made me as a mirror:

Song can be seen in my breast.

From Ali's face the Prophet drew many a
fair omen,   975

By his majesty the true religion is glorified.

His commandments are the strength of Islam:

All things pay allegiance to his House.

The Apostle of God gave him the name Bu Turab;

God in the Qur'ān called him "the Hand

of Allah."   **980**

Every one that is acquainted with Life's mysteries

Knows what is the inner meaning of the names of Ali.

The dark clay, whose name is the body—

Our reason is ever be-moaning its iniquity.

On account of it our sky-reaching thought plods

o'er the earth;   **985**

It makes our eyes blind and our ears deaf.

It hath in its hand a two-edge sword of lust:

Travellers' hearts are broken by this brigand.

Ali, the Lion of God, subdued the body's clay

And transmuted this dark earth to gold.   **990**

Murtaza, by whose sword the splendour of Truth was
revealed,

Is named Bu Turab from his conquest of the body.[1]

Man wins territory by prowess in battle,

But his brightest jewel is masters of himself.

Whosoever in the world become a Bû Turâb **995**

Turns back the sun from the west;[2]

Whosoever saddles tightly the seed of the body

Sits like the bazel on the seal of sovereignty:

Here the might of Khaibar is under his feet,[3]

And hereafter his hand will distribute the
water of Kauthar.[4] **1000**

Through self-knowledge he acts as God's Hand,

And in virtue of being God's Hand he reigns over all.

His person is the gate of the city of the sciences.[5]

Arabia, China, and Greece are subject to him.

If thou wouldst drink clear wine from
thine own grapes, **1005**

Thou must needs wield authority over thine own earth.

To become earth is the creed of a moth:

---

2. A miracle attributed to Ali.

3. The fortress of Khaibar, a village in the Hijāz, was captured by the Muslims in A.D. 628. Ali performed great facts of valour on this occasion.

4. A river of Paradise.

5. According to the Tradition of the Prophet, "I am the city of Knowledge and Ali is the gate."

Be a conqueror of earth; that alone is worthy of a man.

Thou art soft as a rose. Become hard as a stone,

That thou mayst be the foundation of the wall
    of the garden!   **1010**

Build thy clay into a Man,

Build thy Man into a World!

Unless from thine own earth thou build thine
    own wall or door.

Someone else will make bricks of thine earth.

O thou who complaisant of the cruelty
    of Heaven,   **1015**

Thou whose glass cries out against the injustice of
    the stone,

How long this weiling and crying and lamentation?

How long this perpetual beating of thy breast?

The pith of Life is contained in action,

The delight in creation is the law of Life.   **1020**

Arise and create a new world!

Wrap thyself in flames, be an Abraham![6]

To comply with this world which does not favour thy
    purposes

---

6. See not on 1,213.

Is to fling away thy buckler on the field of battle.

The man of strong character who is master
     of himself   **1025**

Will find Fortune complaisant.

If the world does not comply with his humour,

He will try the hazard of war with Heaven:

He will dig up the foundations of the universe

And cast its atoms into a new mould.   **1030**

He will subvert the course of Time

And wreck the azure firmament.

By his own strength he will produce

A new world which will do his pleasure.

If one cannot live in the world as be-seems
     a man,   **1035**

Then it is better to die like the brave.

He that hath a sound heart

Will prove his strength by great enterprises.

'Tis sweet to use love in hard tasks

And, like Abrãham, to gether roses from
     flames.[7]   **1040**

---

7. The burning pyre on which Abraham was thrown lost its heat and
was transformed into a rose-garden.

The potentialities of men of action

Are displayed in willing acceptance of what is
    difficult.

Mean spirits have no weapon but resentment,

Life has only one law.

Life is power made manifest,   **1045**

And its mainspring is the desire for victory.

Mercy out of season is a chilling of Life's blood,

A break in the rhythm of Life's music.

Whoever is sunk in the depths of ignominy

Calls his weakness contentment.   **1050**

Weakness is the plunderer of Life,

Its womb is teeming with fears and lies.

Its soul is empty of virtues,

Vices fatten on its milk.

O man of sound judgement, beware!   **1055**

This spoiler is lurking in ambush

Be not its dupe, if thou art wise:

Chameleon-like, it changes colour every moment.

Even by keen observers its form is not discerned:

Veils are thrown over its face.   **1060**

Now it is muffled in pity and gentleness,

Now it wears the cloak of humanity.

Sometimes it is disguised as compulsion,

Sometimes as excusability.

It appears in the shape of self-indulgence   **1065**

And robs the strong man's heart of courage.

Strength is the twin of Truth;

If thou knowest thyself, strength is the Truth-
    revealing glass.

Life is the seed, and power the crop:

Power explains the mystery of truth and
    falsehood.   **1070**

A claimant, if he be possessed of power,

Needs no argument for his claim.

Falsehood derives from power the authority of truth,

And by falsifying truth deems itself true.

Its creative word transforms poison
    into nectar.   **1075**

It says to good, "Thou art bad," and Good
    becomes Evil.

O thou that art heedless of the trust committed to thee,

Esteem thyself superior to both worlds![8]

---

8. The "trust" which God offered to Man and which Man accepted,
after it had been refused by Heaven and Earth (Qur'ān. ch. 33, v. 72), is
the divine vicegerency, *i.e.*, the duty of displaying the divine attributes.

Gain knowledge of Life's mysteries!

Be a tyrant! Ignore all except God   **1080**

O man of understanding, open thine eyes, ears,
    and lips![9]

If then thou seest not the Way of Truth, laugh at me!

---

9. A parody of the verse in the *Masnavî* quoted above. See 1,603.

word misused

11

STORY OF A YOUNG MAN OF MERV WHO CAME TO THE SAINT ALI HUJWIRI—GOD HAVE MERCY ON HIM!—AND COMPLAINED THAT HE WAS OPPRESSED BY HIS ENEMIES

THE saint of Hujwir was venerated by the peoples,

And Pîr-i-Sanjar visited his tomb as a pilgrim.[1]

With ease he broke down the mountain-
barries   **1085**

And sowed the seed of Islam in India.

The age of Omar was restored by his godliness.

The fame of the Truth was exalted by his words.

He was a guardian of the honour of the Qur'ãn.

The house of Falsehood fell in ruins
at his gaze.   **1090**

---

1. Hujwîrî author of the oldest Persian treatise on Sûfism, was a native of Ghazna in Afghanistan. He died at Lahore about A.D. 1072 Pîr-i-Sanjar is the renowned saint, Mu'înuddîn, head of the Chishti order of dervishes, who died in A.D. 1235 at Ajmîr.

The dust of the Punjab was brought to life by his
    breath,

Our dawn was made splendid by his sun.

He was a lover, and withal, a courier of Love:

The secrets of Love shone forth from his brow.

I will tell a story of his perfection   **1095**

And enclose a whole rose-bed in a single bud.

A young man, cypress-tall,

Came from the town of Merve to Lahore.

He went to see the venerable saint,

That the sun might dispth is darkness.   **1100**

"I am hemmed in," he said, "by foes;

I am as a glass in the midst of stones.

Do thou teach me, O sire of heavenly rank,

How to lead my life amongst enemies!"

The wise Director, in whose nature   **1105**

Love had allied beauty with majesty,

Answered: "Thou art unread in Life's lore,

Careless of its end and its beginning.

Be without fear of others!

Thou art a sleeping force: awake!   **1110**

When the stone thought itself to be glass,

It became glass and got into the way of breaking.

If the traveller thinks himself weak,

He delivers his soul unto the brigand.

How long wilt thou regard thyself as
　　water and clay?　　　　　　　　　　**1115**

Create from thy clay a flaming Sinai!

Why be angry with mighty men?

Why complain of enemies?

I will declare the truth: thine enemy is thy friend:

His existence crowns thee with glory.　　**1120**

Whosoever knows the states of the Self

Considers a powerful enemy to be blessing
　　from God.

To the seed of Man the enemy is as a rain-cloud:

He awakens its potentialities.

If thy spirit be strong, the stones in thy way
　　are as water:　　　　　　　　　　**1125**

What recks the torrent of the ups and downs
　　of the road?

The sword of resolution is whetted by the
　　stones in the way

And put to proof by traversing stage after stage.

What is the use of eating and sleeping like a beast?

What is the use of being, unless thou have
    strength in thyself?   **1130**

When thou mak'st thyself strong with Self,

Thou wilt destroy the world at thy pleasure.

If thou wouldst pass away, become free of Self;

If thou wouldst live, become full of Self![2]

Who is death? To become oblivious to Self.   **1135**

Why imagine that it is the parting of soul and body?

Abide in Self, like Joseph?

Advance from captivity to empire!

Think of Self and be a man of action

Be a man of God, bear mysteries within!"   **1140**

I will explain the matter by means of stories,

I will open the bud by the power of my breath.

"'Tis better that a lover's secret

Should be told by the lips of others."[3]

---

2. These lines correct the Sufi doctrine that means of passing away
from individuality the mystic attains to everlasting life in God.

3. *I.e.*, allegorically. This verse occurs in the *Masnaví*.

diamond/dewdrop
Self

12

STORY OF THE BIRD THAT WAS FAINT WITH THIRST

A BIRD was faint with thirst,   1145

The breath in his body was heaving like waves of smoke.

He saw a diamond in the garden:

Thirst created a vision of water.

Deceived by the sunbright stone

The foolish bird fancied that it was water.   1150

He got no moisture from the gem:

He pecked it with his beak, but it did not wet his palate.

"O thrall of vain desire," said the diamond.

"Thou hast sharpened thy greedy beak on me;

But I am not a dewdrop, I give no drink,   1155

I do not live for the sake of others.

Wouldst thou hurt me? Thou art mad!

A lie that reveals the Self is strange to thee.

My water will shiver the beaks of birds

And break the jewel of man's like."[1]   **1160**

The bird won not his heart's wish from the diamond

And turned away from the sparkling stone.

Disappointment swelled in his breast,

The song in his throat became a wail.

Upon a rose-twig a drop of dew   **1165**

Gleamed like the tear in a nightingale's eye:

All its glitter was owing to the sun,

It was trembling in fear of the sun—

A restless sky-born star

That had stopped for a moment, from desire
    to be seen;   **1170**

Oft deceived by bud and flower,

It had gained nothing from Life.

There it hung, ready to drop.

Like a tear on the eyelashes of a lover who hath lost
    his heart.

The sorely distressed bird hopped under the
    rose-bush.   **1175**

---

1. *I.e.*, if he swallow a diamond, he will die.

The dewdrop trickled into his mouth.

O thou that wouldst deliver thy soul from enemies.

I sake thee— "Art thou a drop of water or a gem?"

When the bird melted in the fire of thirst,

It appropriated the life of another.   **1180**

The drop was not solid and gem-like;

The diamond had a being, the drop had none.

Never for an instant neglect Self-preservation:

Be a diamond, not a dewdrop!

Be massive in nature, like mountains,   **1185**

And bear on thy crest a hundred clouds laden with
     floods of rain!

Save thyself by affirmation of Self,

Compress thy quicksilver into silver ore!

Produce a melody from the string of Self,

Make manifest the secrets of Self!   **1190**

13

STORY OF THE DIAMOND AND THE COAL

NOW I will open one more gate of Truth,
I will tell thee another tale.
The coal in the mine said to the diamond,
"O thou entrusted with splendours ever-lasting.
We are comrades, and our being is one;   1195
The source of our existence is the same,
Yet while I die here in the anguish of worthlessness,
Thou art set on the crowns of emperors.
My stuff is so vile that I am valued less than earth,
Whereas the mirror's heart is rent by
     thy beauty,   1200
My darkness illumines the chafing dish,
Then my substance is incinerated at last
Every one puts the sole of his foot on my head
And covers my stock of existence with ashes.
My fate must needs be deplored: 1205

Dost thou know what is the gist of my being?

It is a condensed wavelet of smoke,

Endowed with a single spark.[1]

Both in feature and nature thou art starlike,

Splendours rise from every side of thee.   **1210**

Now thou become'st the light of a monarch's eye,

Now thou adornest the haft of a danger."

"O sagacious friend!" said the diamond,

"Dark earth, when hardened, becomes in dignity
  as a bezel.

Having been at strife with its environment,   **1215**

It is ripened by the struggle and grows hard
  like a stone.

'Tis this ripeness that has endowed my form with light.

And filled my bossom with radiance.

Because thy being is immature, thou hast become
  abased;

Because thy body is soft, thou art burnt.   **1220**

Be void of fear, grief, and anxiety;

Be hard as a stone, be a diamond!

---

1. These two lines indicate the gist of the coal's being.

Whosoever strives hard and grips tight,

The two worlds are illumined by him.

A little earth is the origin of the Black Stone   **1225**

Which puts forth its head in the Qa'ba:

Its rank is higher than Sinai,

It is kissed by the swarthy and the fair.

In solidity consists the glory of Life:

Weakness is worthlessness and immaturity."   **1230**

Long unconvincing lecture!

14

STORY OF THE SHEIKH AND THE BRAHMIN, FOLLOWED BY A CONVERSATION BETWEEN GANGES AND HIMALAYAS TO THE EFFECT THAT THE CONTINUATION OF SOCIAL LIFE DEPENDS ON FIRM ATTACHMENTS TO THE CHARACTERISTIC TRADITIONS OF THE COMMUNITY

AT Benares lived a venerable Brahmin,

Whose head was deep in the ocean of Being and
    Not-being.

He had a large knowledge of philosophy

But was well-disposed to the seekers after God.

His mind was eager to explore new problems, **1235**

His intellect moved on a level with the Pleiades;

His nest was as high as that of the Anka;[1]

---

1. A mysterious bird, of which nothing is known except its name.

Sun and moon were cast, like rue, on the flame of his
    thought.[2]

For a long time he laboured and sweated,

But philosophy brought no wine to his cup.   **1240**

Although he set many a snare in the gardens of
    learning,

His snares never caught a glimpse of the Ideal bird;

And notwithstanding that the nails of his thought were
    dabbled with blood,

The knot of Being and Not-being remained united.

The sighs on his lips bore witness to his
    despair,   **1245**

His countenance told tales of his distraction.

One day he visited an excellent Sheikh,

A man who had in his breast a heart of gold.

The Brahmin laid the seal of silence on his lips.

And lent his ear to the Sage's discourse.   **1250**

Then said the Sheikh: "O wanderer in the lofty sky!

Pledge thyself to be true, for a little, to the earth!

Thou hast lost thy way in wildernesses of speculation,

---

2. Rue-seed is burned for the purpose of fumigation.

Thy fearless thought hath passed beyond Heaven.

Be reconciled with earth, O sky-traveller!   **1255**

Do not wander in quest of the essence of the stars!

I do not did thee abandon thine idols.

Art thou an unbeliever? Then be worthy of the badge
 of unbelief![3]

O inheritor of ancient culture,

Turn not thy back on the path thy fathers trod!**1260**

If a people's life is derived from unity,

Unbelief too is source of unity.

Thou that art not even a perfect infidel,

Art unfit to worship at the shrine of the spirit.

We both are far astray from the road
 of devotion: **1265**

Thou art far from Azar, and I from Abraham.[4]

Our Majnun hath not fallen into melancholy for his
 Laila's sake:

He hath not become perfect in the madness of love.

When the lamp of Self-expires,

---

3. "The badge of unbelief": here the original has *sunnār* (*Zwvāpioû*)
i.e., the sacred thread worn by Zoroastrians and other non-Muslims.

4. Azar, the father of Abraham, was an idolater.

What is the use of heaven surveying
    imagination?"   **1270**

Once on a time, laying hold of the skirt of the
    mountain,

Ganges said to Himalaya:

"O thou mantled in snow since the morn of creation,

Thou whose form is girdled with streams,

God made thee a partner in the secrets
    of heaven.   **1275**

But deprived thy foot of graceful gait.

He took away from thee the power to walk:

What avails this sublimity and stateliness?

Life springs from perpetual movement;

Motion constitutes the wave's whole
    existence,"   **1280**

When the mountain heard this taunt from the river,

He puffed angrily like a sea of fire,

And answered: "Thy wide waters are my looking-
    glass;

Within my bosom are a hundred rivers like thee.

This graceful gait of thine is an instrument
    of death: **1285**

Whoso goeth from Self is meet to die.

Thou hast no knowledge of thine own case,

Thou exultest in thy mis-fortune: thou art a fool!

O born of the womb of the revolving sky,

A fallen-in bank is better than thou!   **1290**

Thou hast made thine existence an offering
  to the ocean,

Thou hast thrown the rich purse of thy life
  to the highway man.

Be self-contained like the rose in the garden,

Do not go to the florist in order to spread thy perfume!

To live is to grow in thyself   **1295**

And gather roses from thine own flower-bed.

Ages have gone by and my foot is fast on earth,

Dost thou fancy that I am far from my goal?

My being grew and reached the sky,

The Pleiads sank to rest under my skirts;   **1300**

Thy being vanishes in the ocean,

But on my crest the stars bow their heads.

Mine eye sees the mysteries of heaven,

Mine ear is familiar with angels' wings.

Since I glowed with the heat of
    unceasing toll,   **1305**

I amassed rubies, diamonds, and other gems.

I am stone within, and in the stone is fire:

Water cannot pass over my fire!"

Art thou a drop of water? Do not break at
    thine own feet.

But endeavour to surge and wrestle with
    the sea.   **1310**

Desire the water of a jewel, become a jewel!

Be an ear-drop, adorn a beauty!

Oh, expand thyself! Move swiftly!

Be a cloud that shoots lightning and sheds a
    flood of rain!

Let the ocean sue for thy storms as a beggar,   **1315**

Let it complain of the straitness of its skirts!

Let it deem itself less than a wave

And glide alone at thy feet!

15

SHOWING THAT THE PURPOSE OF THE MUSLIM'S LIFE IS TO EXALT THE WORD OF ALLAH, AND THAT THE JIHĀD (WAR AGAINST UNBELIEVERS), IF IT BE PROMPTED BY LAND-HUNGER, IS UNLAWFUL IN THE RELIGION OF ISLAM

IMBUE thine heart with the tincture of Allah,

Give honour and glory to Love!   **1320**

The Muslim's nature prevails by means of love.

The Muslim, if he be not loving, is an infidel.

Upon God depends his seeing and not seeing,

His eating, drinking, and sleeping.

In his will that which God wills

    becomes lost—   **1325**

"How shall a man believe this saying?"[1]

He encamps in the field of "There is no god but Allah";

---

1. See Introduction, p. xix, note 1.

In the world he is a witness to mankind.[2]

His high estate is attested by the Prophet who
    was sent to men and Jinn—

The most truthful of witnesses.   **1330**

Leave words and seek that spiritual state,

Shed the light of God o'er the darkness of thy deeds!

Albeit clad in kingly robe, live as a dervish,

Live wakeful and meditating on God!

Whatever thou dost, let it be thine aim therein
    to draw nigh to God,   **1335**

That his glory may be made manifest by thee

Peace becomes an evil, if its object be aught else;

War is good if its object is God.

If God be not exalted by our swords.

War dishonours the people.   **1340**

The holy Sheikh Miyan Mir Wali,[3]

By the light of whose soul every hidden
    thing was revealed—

His feet were firmly planted on the path of
    Muhammad,

---

2. *I.e.*, that life of the true Muslim displays to mankind the ideal realised.

3. A celebrated Muslim saint, who died at Lahore in A.D. 1635.

He was a flute for the impassioned music of love.

His tomb keeps our city safe from harm   **1345**

And causes the beams of true religion to shine on us.

Heaven stooped its brow to his threshold,

The Emperor of India was one of his disciples.[4]

Now, this monarch had sown the seed of
    ambition in his heart

And was resolved on conquest.   **1350**

The flames of vain desire were alight in him,

He was teaching his sword to ask, "Is there
    any more?"[5]

In the Deccan was a great noise of war,

His army stood on the battle-field.

He went to the Sheikh of heaven-high dignity **1355**

That he might receive his blessing:

The Muslim turns from this world to God

And strengthens policy with prayer.

The Sheikh made no answer to the Emperor's speech,

The assembly of dervishes was all ears,   **1360**

Until a disciple, in his hand a silver coin,

---

4. Shah Jahan

5. Qur'ān, ch. 50 v. 29.

Opened his lips and broke the silence,

Saying, "Accept this poor offering from me,

O guide of them that have lost the way to God!

My limbs were bathed in sweat of labour   **1365**

Before I put away a dirhem in my skirt."

The Sheikh said: "This money ought to be
    given to our Sultan,

Who is a beggar wearing the raiment of a king.

Though he holds sway over sun, moon, and stars,

Our Emperor is the most penniless
    of mankind.   **1370**

His eye is fixed on the table of strangers,

The fire of his hunger hath consumed a whole world.

His sword is followed by famine and plague,

His building lays a wide had waste.

The folk are crying out because of
    his indigence;   **1375**

His empty-handedness causes him to plunder
    the weak.

His power is an enemy to all:

Humankind are the caravan and he the brigand.

In his self-delusion and ignorance

He calls pillage by the name of empire   **1380**

Both the royal troops and those of the enemy

Are cloven in twain by the sword of his hunger.

The beggar's hunger consumes his own soul,

But the Sultan's hunger destroys state and religion.

Whoso shall draw the sword for anything
    except Allah,   **1385**

His sword is sheathed in his own breast."

16

PRECEPTS WRITTEN FOR THE MUSLIMS OF INDIA BY MIR NAJAT NAKSHBANDI, WHO IS GENERALLY KNOWN AS BÃBÃ SAHRÃ'I[1]

O THOU that hast grown from earth, like a rose,

Thou too art born of the womb of Self.

Do not a band on Self! Persist therein!

Be a drop of water and drink up the ocean!   **1390**

Glowing with the light of Self as thou art,

Make Self strong, and thou with endure.

Thou gett'st profit from the trade,

Thou gain'st riches by preserving this commodity.

Thou art Being, and art thou afraid of
not-being?   **1395**

Dear friend, thy understanding is at fault.

Since I am acquainted with the harmony of Life.

---

1. This appear's to be a pseudonym assumed by the author.

I will tell thee what is the secret of Life—

To sink into thyself like the pearl,

Then to emerge from thine inward solitude;   **1400**

To collect sparks beneath the ashes,

And become a flame and dazzle men's eyes.

Go, burn the house of forty years' tribulation,

Move round thyself! By a circling flame!

What is Life but to be freed from moving
     round others   **1405**

And to regard thyself as the Holy Temple?

Beat thy wings and escape from the attraction of Earth:

Like birds be safe from falling.

Unless thou art a bird, thou wilt do wisely

Not to build thy nest on the top of a cave.   **1410**

O thou that seekest to acquire knowledge,

I say o'er to thee the message of the Sage of Rum:[2]

"Knowledge, if it lie on thy skin, is a snake;

Knowledge, if thou take it to heart, is a friend."

Hast thou heard how the Master of Rum   **1415**

Gave lectures on philosophy at Aleppo?—

---

2. Jalālu'ddin Rûmî.

Fast in the bonds of intellectual proofs,

Drifting o'er the dark and stormy sea of understanding;

A Moses unillumined by Love's Sinai,

Ignorant of Love and of Love's passion.   **1420**

He discoursed on Scepticism and Neoplatonism,

And strung many a brilliant pearl of metaphysic.

He unravelled the problems of the Peripatetics,

The light of his thought made clear whatever
        was obscure.

Heaps of books lay around and in
        front of him,   **1425**

And on his lips was the key to all their mysteries.

Shams-i-Tabriz, directed by Kamal,[3]

Sought his way to the college of Jalāu'ddin Rūmî

And cried out, "What is all this noise and babble?

What are these syllogisms and judgements
        and demonstrations?"   **1430**

"Peace, O fool!" exclaimed the Maulvi,

"Do not laugh at the doctrines of the sages.

Get thee out of my college!

---

3. Bābā Kamaluddin Jundî. For Shams-i-Tabrîz and his relation to
Jalālu'ddin Rūmî see my *Selected Poems from the Divān-i-Shams-i-
Tabriz* (Cambridge, 1898).

This is argument and discussion: what hast thou
    to do with it?

My discourse is beyond thy understanding.   **1435**

It brightens the glass of perception."

These words increased the anger of Shams-i-Tabrîz

And caused a fire to burst forth from his soul.

The lightning of his look fell on the earth,

And the glow of his breath made the dust
    spring into flames.   **1440**

The spiritual fire burned the intellectual stack

And clean consumed the library of the philosopher.

The Maulvi, being a stranger to Love's miracles

And unversed in Love's harmonies,

Cried, "How didst thou kindle this fire,   **1445**

Which hath burned the books of the philosophers?"

The Sheikh answered, "O unbelieving Muslim,

This is vision and ecstasy: what hast thou to
    do with it?

My state is beyond thy thought,

My flame is the Alchemist's elixir,"   **1450**

Thou hast drawn thy substance from the snow of
    philosophy,

The cloud of thy thought sheds nothing but hailstones.

Kindle a fire in thy rubble,

Foster a flame in thy earth!

The Muslim's knowledge is perfected by spiritual
    fervour,   **1455**

The meaning of Islam is *Renounce what shall pass
    away.*

When Abraham escaped from the bondage of "that
    which sets,"[4]

He sat unhurt in the midst of flames.[5]

Thou hast cast knowledge of God behind thee

And squandered thy religion for the sake
    of a loaf.   **1460**

Thou art hot in pursuit of antimony,

Thou art unaware of the blackness of thine own eye.

Seek the Fountain of Life from the sword's edge.

And the River of Paradise from the dragon's mouth.

Demand the Black Stone from the door of
    the house of idols.   **1465**

---

4. Abraham refused to worship the sun, moon, and stars, saying, "I love not them that set" (Qur'ān, ch. 6, v. 76).

5. See p. 91, note.

And the musk-deer's bladder from a mad dog,

But do no seek the glow of Love from the
    knowledge of today,

Do not seek the nature of Truth from this
    infidel's cup!

Long have I been running to and fro,

Learning the secrets of the New Knowledge: **1470**

Its gardeners have put me to the trial

And have made me intimate with their roses.

Roses! Tulips, rather, that warn one not to
    smell them—

Like paper roses, a mirage of perfume.

Since this garden ceased to enthrall me **1475**

I have nested on the Paradisal tree.

Modern knowledge is the greatest blind—

Idol-worshipping, idol-selling, idol-making!

Shackled in the prison of phenomena,

It has not overleaped the limits of
    the sensible. **1480**

It has fallen down in crossing the bridge of Life,

It has laid the knife to its own throat.

Its fire is cold as the flame of the tulip;

Its flames are frozen like hail.

Its nature remains untouched by the glow
of Love,   **1485**

It is ever engaged in joyless search.

Love is the Plato that heals the sicknesses of the mind:[6]

The mind's melancholy is cured by its lancet.

The whole world bows in adoration to Love,

Love is the Mahmud that conquers the
Somnath of intellect.[7]   **1490**

Modern science lacks this old wine in its cup,

Its nights are not loud with passionate prayer.

Thou hast misprized thine own cypress

And deemed tall the cypress of others.

Like the reed, thou hast emptied thyself
of Self.   **1495**

And given thine heart to the music of others,

O thou that begg'st morsels from an other's table.

Wilt thou seek thine own kind in another's shop?

---

6. In the *Masnavi* Love is called "the physician of our pride and self-conceit, our Plato, and our Galen."

7. The famous idol of Somnath was destroyed by Sultan Mahmud of Ghazna.

The Muslim's assembly-place is burned up by the
    lamps of strangers,

His mosque is consumed by the sparks
    of monasticism.   **1500**

When the deer fled from the sacred territory
    of Makkah,

The hunter's arrow pierced her side.[8]

The leaves of the rose are scattered like its scent:

O thou that has fled from the Self, come back to it:

O trustee of the wisdom of the Qur'ān   **1505**

Find the lost unity again!

We, who keep the gate of the citadel of Islam,

Have become unbelievers by neglecting the
    watchword of Islam.

The ancient Saki's bowl is shattered,

The wine-party of the Hijaz is broken up.   **1510**

The Qa'ba is filled with our idols,

Infidelity mocks at our Islam.

Our Sheikh hath gambled Islam away for love of idols.

And made a rosary of the *zunnar*.[9]

---

8. The pilgrims are forbidden to kill game.
9. See p. 10, note.

Our spiritual directors owe their rank to
    their white hairs   **1515**

And are the laughing-stock of children in the street;

Their hearts bear no impress of the Faith

But house the idols of sensuality.

Every long-haired fellow wears the garb of a dervish—

Alas for these traffickers in religion! *like him* **1520**

Day and night they are travelling about with disciples,

Insensible to the great needs of Islam.

Their eyes are without light, like the narcissus.

Their breasts devoid of spiritual wealth.

Preachers and Sufis, all worship
    worldliness alike;   **1525**

The prestige of the pure religion is ruined.

Our preacher fixed his eyes on the pagoda

And the mufti of the Faith sold his verdict.

After this, O friends, what are we to do?

Our guide turns his face towards the
    wine-house.   **1530**

17

TIME IS A SWORD

GREEN be the holy grave of Shafi'i,[1]
Whose vine hath cheered a whole world?
His thought plucked a star from heavens:
He named time "a cutting sword."
How shall I say what is the secret of
    this sword?   **1535**
In its flashing edge there is life.
Its owner is exalted above hope and fear.
His hand is whiter than the hand of Moses.
At one stroke thereof water gushes from the rock
And the sea becomes land from dearth
    of moisture.   **1540**
Moses held this sword in his hand,
Therefore he wrought more than man may contrive.

---

1. Founder of one of the four great Mohammadan schools of law.

He clove the Red Sea asunder

And made its waters like dry earth.

The arm of Ali, the conqueror of Khaibar,   **1545**

Drew its strength from this same sword.

The revolution of the sky is worth seeing,

The change of day and night is worth observing.[2]

Look, O thou enthralled by Yesterday and To-morrow,

Behold another world in thine on heart!   **1550**

Thou hast sown the seed of darkness in the clay,

Thou hast imagined Time as a line.

Thy thought measures length of Time

With the measure of night and day.

Thou mak'st this line a girdle on thine
    infidel waist;   **1555**

Thou art an advertiser of falsehood, like idols.

Thou wert the Elixir, and thou hast become a
    peck of dust;

Thou wert born the conscience of Truth, and
    thou hast become a lie!

Art thou a Muslim? Then cast of this girdle!

---

2. *I.e.*, turn you attention to the nature and meaning of Time.

Be a candle to the feast of the religion of
    the free!   **1560**

Knowing not the origin of Time,

Thou art ignorant of everlasting Life.

How long wilt thou be a thrall of night and day?

Learn the mystery of Time from the words "I
    have a time with God."[3]

Phenomena arise from the march of Time,   **1565**

Life is one of Time's mysteries.

The cause of Time is not the revolution of the sun:

Time is everlasting, but the sun does not last for ever.

Time is joy and sorrow, festival and fast,

Time is the secret of moonlight and sunlight. **1570**

Thou hast extended Time, like Space,

And distinguished Yesterday from Tomorrow.

Thou hast fled like a scent, from thine own garden;

Thou hast made thy prison with thine own hand.

Our time which has neither beginning
    nor end,   **1575**

---

3. The Prophet said, "I have a time with God of such sort that neither
angel nor Prophet is my peer," meaning (if we interpret his words
according to the sense of this passage) that he felt himself to be timeless.

The Prophet → Timeless.)

Blossoms from the flower-bed of our mind.

To know its root quickens the living with new life:

Its being is more splendid than the dawn.

Life is of Time, and Time is of Life:

"Do not abuse time!" was the command of
    the Prophet.[4]   **1580**

Oh, the memory of those days when Time's sword

Was allied with the strength of our hands![5]

We sowed the seed of religion in men's hearts

And unveiled the face of Truth;

Our nails tore loose the knot of this world,   **1585**

Our bowing in prayer gives blessings to the earth.

From the jar of Truth we made rosy wine gush forth,

We charged against the ancient taverns.

O thou in whose cup is old wine

A wine so hot that the glass is well-nigh
    turned to water,   **1590**

Wilt thou in thy pride and arrogance and self-conceit

---

4. The Prophet is reported to have said, "Do not abuse Time, for
Time is God."

5. The glorious days when Islam first set out to convert and conquer
the world.

Taunt us with our emptiness?

Our cup, too, hath graced the symposium;

Our breast hath owned a spirit.

The new age with all its glories   **1595**

Hath risen from the dust of our feet.

Our blood hath watered God's harvest,

All worshippers of God are our debtors.

The *takbir* was our gift to the world,[6]

Qa'bas were built of our clay.   **1600**

By means of us God taught the Qur'ān,

From our hand He dispensed His bounty.

Although crown and signet have passed from us,

Do not look with contempt on our beggarliness!

In thine eyes we are good for nothing,   **1605**

Thinking old thoughts, despicable.

We have honour from "There is no god but Allah,"

We are the protectors of the universe.

Freed from the vexation of to-day and to-morrow.

We have pledged ourselves to love One.   **1610**

We are the conscience hidden in God's heart,

---

6. The *takbir* is the cry "*Allah akbar*," "Allah is most great."

We are the heirs of Moses and Aaron,
Sun and moon are still bright with our radiance,
Lightning-flashes still lurk in our cloud.
In our essence Divinity is mirrored: **1615**
The Muslim's being is one of the signs of God.

Aaron

18

AN INVOCATION

O THOU that art as the soul in the body of the universe,

Thou art our soul end thou art ever fleeing from us.

Thou breathest music into Life's lute;

Life envies Death when death is for thy sake   **1620**

One more bring comfort to our sad hearts,

Once more dwell in our breasts!

Once more demand from us the sacrifice of name and
   fame,

Strengthen our weak love.

We are off complaining of destiny,   **1625**

Thou art of great price and we have naught.

Hide not thy fair face from the empty-handed!

Sell cheap the love of Salman and Bilal![1]

Give us the sleepless eye and the passionate heart,

---

1. Salman was a Persian, Bilal an Abyssinian. Both had been slaves
and were devoted benchmen of the Prophet.

Give us again the nature of quick-silver!   **1630**

Show unto us one of thy manifest signs,

That the necks of our enemies may be bowed!

Make this chaff a mountain crested with fire,

Burn with our fire all that is not God!

When the people of Islam let the thread of Unity
  go from their hands,   **1635**

They fell into a hundred mazes.

We are dispersed like stars in the world;

Though of the same family, we are strange
  to one another.

Bind again these scattered leaves,

Revive the law of love!   **1640**

Take us back to serve thee as of old,

Commit thy cause to them that love thee!

We are travellers: give us resignation as our goal!

Give us the strong faith of Abraham!

Make us know the meaning of "There
  is no God."   **1645**

Make us acquainted with the mystery of
  "except Allah!"[2]

---

2. *I.e.*, affirmation of the Divine Unity.

I who burn like a candle for the sake of others

Teach myself to weep like that candle.

O God! a tear that is heart-enkindling,

Passionful, wrung forth by pain, peace-
    consuming, **1650**

May I sow in the garden, and may it grow into a fire

That washes away the fire-brand from the tulip's robe!

My heart is with yestereve, my eye is on tomorrow:

Amidst the company I am alone.

"Every one fancies he is my friend, **1655**

But none ever sought the secrets within my soul."

Oh, where in the wide world is my comrade?

I am the Bush of Sinai: where is my Moses?

I am tyrannous, I have done many a wrong to myself,

I have nourished a flame in my bosom, **1660**

A flame that burnt to ashes the wares of understanding,

Cast fire on the skirt of discretion,

Lessened with madness the proud reason,

And inflamed the very being of knowledge:

Its blaze enthrones the sun in the sky **1665**

And lightnings encircle it with adoration for ever.

Mine eye fell to weeping, like dew,

Since I was entrusted with that hidden fire.

I taught the candle to burn openly,

While I myself burned unseen by the
  world's eye.   **1670**

As last flames burst forth from every hair of me,

Fire dropped from the veins of my thought:

My nightingale picked up the spark grains

And created a fire-tempered song.

The breast of this age is without a heart,   **1675**

Majnun quivers with pain because Laila's
  howdah is empty.

It is not easy for the candle to throb alone;

Ah, is there no moth worthy of me?

How long shall I wait for one to share my grief?

How long must I search for a confidant?   **1680**

O Thou whose face lends light to the moon and the
  stars,

Withdraw Thy fire from soul!

Take back what Thou hast put in my breast,

Remove the stabbing radiance from my mirror,

Or give me one old comrade **1685**

To be the mirror of mine all-burning love!

In the sea wave tosses side by side with wave:

Each hath a partner in its emotion.

In heaven star consorts with star.

And the bright moon lays her head on the
    knees of Night. **1690**

Morning touches Night's dark side,

And To-day throws itself against To-morrow

One river loses its being in another,

A waft of air dies in perfume.

There is dancing in every nook of the
    wilderness. **1695**

Madman dances with madman.

Because in thine essence Thou art single,

Thou hast evolved for Thyself a whole world,

I am as the tulip of the field,

In the midst of a company I am alone. **1700**

I beg of Thy grace a sympathising friend,

And adept in the mysteries of my nature,

A friend endowed with madness and wisdom,

One that knoweth not the phantom of vain things,

That I may confide my lament to his soul   **1705**

And see again my face in his heart.

His image I will mould of mine own clay,

I will be to him both idol and worshipper.